HAVE YOU MET MONEY?

Everything you need to get started

DAVID LEHMAN

Copyright © 2022 – DAVID LEHMAN

All rights to this book are reserved. No permission is given for any part of this book to be reproduced, transmitted in any form or means; electronic or mechanical, stored in a retrieval system, photocopied, recorded, scanned, or otherwise. Any of these actions require the proper written permission of the author.

Table of Contents

WHAT YOU NEED TO KNOW ABOUT THIS BOOK

HAVE YOU MET MONEY?

Chapter One: WHERE TO START?

- Mindset about money
- Modalities regarding money
- Purpose of money
- Managing expectations about money
- Understanding the risks of money
- One man's debt are another man's assets
- Make SMART goals
- Financial Responsibility

Chapter Two: WHAT IS MONEY?

- Currency
- Fiat Currency
- Hard money
- Bullion
- Bars
- Rounds
- Precious Metals
- Noble Metals
- U.S. Dollar index
- Mining
- Minting
- Mintages
- Coins

Table of Contents

Error Coins
Proof Coins
Numismatics
Cull coin
Constitutional Silver
Personal Financial Statement
Barter

Chapter Three: HOW DOES MONEY WORK?

IRS
Central Bank
Federal Reserves
Strategies
Systems
Methodology
Modalities
Buyback Price
Rate of decay
Taxes
Charting
Economics
Economic growth
Economic collapse
Macroeconomics
Microeconomics
Capitalism
Supply and Demand law
Gold silver ratio
Mint ratio
Assets
Liabilities

Commodity
Investment Vehicle
Investment Time Horizon
Financial Statement
Asset management
Market makers
Market manipulation

Chapter Four: HOW DOES MONEY MOVE?

Capital
Leverage
Liquidity
Patterns
Bears
Bulls
Investment Instruments
Equities
Fort knox
Inflation
Hyper-Inflation
Stagflation
Deflation
Depreciation
Erosion
Volatility
Alerts vs signals vs triggers

Chapter Five: HOW DO I USE MONEY?

Infinite Returns
Types of accounts
Average Dollar costs

Table of Contents

Portfolio
Portfolio weighting
Portfolio diversification
Physical Portfolio
No one knows the future
Entry planning
Short term planning
Market makers
Feasibility study
Market price
Spot price
Premiums
Greshams law
72 rule
Relative value
Intrinsic value
Rate of return
Velocity of money
Zero sum game
Investment time horizon
Diversification
Asset management
Compound Annual growth Rate
Compound Interest
Due diligence
Return on Investment
Opportunity Cost
Tax loss harvesting
Risk management in finance
Ratio of total debts to total assets
Personal Financial plan

REFERENCES

WHAT YOU NEED TO KNOW ABOUT THIS BOOK

I f only there were a required course in high school or college to educate students about the frequently-confusing world of personal finance or at the very least, a cheat sheet distributed at graduation with a list of the most prevalent money traps 20-somethings fall victim to.

Unfortunately, when entering the "real world," most young adults find themselves independently, without guidance about money management. It's time to play Monday morning quarterback and review some of the fundamental money problems many of us in our 30s and 40s wish we had known in our 20s.

HAVE YOU MET MONEY?

Most people in their twenties have a limited budget and little room for frills but when it comes to retirement savings, enabling your money to grow is equally as vital as the money itself.

Consider that your money is more valuable today than it ever will be. Because of the power of compound interest, $1 invested at age 20 will be worth 1.75 times more than $1 invested at age 30, 3.5 times more than $1 invested at age 40 and seven times more than $1 invested at age 50. (assuming an 8 percent rate of return and retirement age of 65).

In addition, many employers will match your retirement contribution, which is practically free money.

I understand that health insurance is not alluring. It is not even material but if you find yourself in the hospital without health insurance, you can face early financial disaster. If you are not insured by your school or work, you should consider getting your health insurance.

The new Affordable Care Act permits you to remain on your parents' insurance until the age of 26 (beginning in the fall of 2010). Some insurance companies provide plans for cash-strapped twenty something.

If you attended college, you should already be accustomed to this way of life. Why not extend the period of frugality by a few years? You can save more money for your future if you live frugally.

Consider staying with your parents a little longer, driving your beat-up car for another year and avoiding additional monthly bills for things you don't need.

When you're barely getting by, it's difficult to consider conserving money. However, if you have an emergency savings account, you can prevent financial difficulty if you lose your job, experience a costly car repair or incur a large unforeseen expense.

Remember that this is a separate fund from your retirement savings. This one is for emergencies, while the other is for your future and is therefore off-limits until that time.

When you're living on Ramen noodles, no one expects you to save thousands of dollars but even a tiny amount can build up over time.

Just because you are eligible for credit does not imply you must accept every offer. You do not need five or ten retail store credit cards.

I understand how enticing it is to take advantage of the "10% off your purchase today" deals that retail establishments frequently advertise. Still, these credit cards typically have hefty interest rates and fees. Now is the moment to establish a credit history. Start with one card and always pay your monthly charge on time and in full.

On other occasions, I've been duped by zero-percent balance transfer promises, only to be hit with excessive costs. If you carry a balance on your credit card and want to take advantage of a cheaper interest rate on another card, read the fine print. Frequently, balance transfers incur fees that exceed the amount of money saved.

You should focus on establishing credit in your twenties, not destroying it. Only charge products you can instantly repay on your credit card and avoid making simply the minimum payment - if you develop this practice, you will be in debt for a very long period.

Also, it is essential just to borrow what you need. Even if you are eligible for a large loan - be it a school loan, auto loan or home loan - you should not take on the full amount. Consider what you need to survive and borrow only that amount.

HAVE YOU MET MONEY?

One of the most typical financial blunders made by people in their twenties is incurring too much debt too soon. It is enticing to be able to charge whatever you want, whenever you want.

However, after you discover your mistake, you can spend the remainder of your twenties and, in some situations, most of your thirties paying off your debts. Do not allow this to occur.

By avoiding many of the frequent pitfalls encountered by people in their twenties, you will position yourself for greater financial success and at 30 or 40 years old, you won't think, "If I had known earlier what I know now."
.

Have a pleasant reading experience.

Chapter One:
Where to Start?

Money is one of those topics that cannot be avoided. No matter who you speak with, the topic of money will inevitably come up. Money is a pervasive topic in our lives, whether we are contemplating the state of the national economy or our own personal affairs. However, there are as many responses to the question "how do you feel about money?" as there are individuals.

This is what I refer to as the 'dichotomy of money'; for some individuals, money is materialistic and monetary, while for others, it is spiritual and emotional. A conflict in money-related beliefs; opposing forces or perspectives regarding whether money is beneficial or bad.

I feel it is all about balance and I will elaborate on my thoughts a bit later. I intend to assist you in reevaluating the concept of money.

HAVE YOU MET MONEY?

Typically, we begin by desiring money to realize a dream; nevertheless, as time passes, we face the risk of money becoming the objective and forgetting the original dream. There are several aspects of life that need interior fulfillment that no amount of money can buy.

On the other hand, it would be naive to ignore the fact that there are many positive uses for money. I believe that one of the main concerns is that we feel guilty about wanting money and to be honest, money can cause many problems if it is not managed properly.

After two years, most lottery winners appear to experience some sort of curse that leaves them worse off than before they obtained their riches.

According to experts, it concerns one's views about money.

Most of our beliefs presumably stem from our upbringing.

What did you see as a child regarding money?

We model what we observe. Were there shortages and needs or abundance and plenty of resources?

I recommend paying close attention to your **financial ideals**. If you believe that _"money doesn't grow on trees"_ & _"money is difficult to come by,"_ you will likely have some degree of dread or anxiety around money.

Here are some of my money-related thoughts:

True, money cannot purchase happiness. However, money may enormously boost your power to impact the world positively.

Your pleasure, joy, relationships, health, wellness and equilibrium are not primarily dependent on having money; rather, having money enables you to appreciate these aspects by **_removing the stress connected with financial obligations._**

Respectfully and ethically earned money can enable you to live comfortably, access goods you want/need, provide an education for your children, own a great home, and a reliable vehicle and support your favorite charity, among other things.

Energy is money. There is nothing improper or unclean about money. People who utilize the money to do wrongdoing are responsible for it.

* You deserve success and you can build a prosperous mindset.

If you have developed unfavorable attitudes about money (negative associations), the only way to overcome them is to retrain your thinking about money consciously.

True prosperity, in my view, is a state of equilibrium and accomplishment in all aspects of our lives, including the physical, mental, spiritual and emotional. When your requirements are covered and you have the freedom to experience and appreciate life, that, to me, exemplifies genuine success.

It begins within and if this requirement is not met, it will not manifest externally. If you are not complete on the inside, you will not feel prosperous and wealthy on the exterior, regardless of how much you have.

Consider what you desire for yourself and your life as your assignment. Be specific. Consider what you must do to accomplish this as well. Record your feelings and thoughts about money in a journal.

If necessary, revisit your childhood but be careful to confront the origins of your ideas. Remember that money will not make you truly wealthy unless you comprehend the duality of money.

Cultivating a Wealth-Building Mindset

When it comes to investing, your mindset about money can have a significant impact on your success. Developing the right mindset is crucial for achieving your financial goals and building wealth over the long term. In this chapter, we'll explore the key elements of a successful investing mindset and how you can cultivate one to enhance your financial future.

Understanding the Purpose of Money

To develop a successful investing mindset, it's important to start by understanding the purpose of money. Money is a tool that can be used to achieve your goals, whether they're related to financial security, providing for your family, or pursuing your passions. Viewing money as a means to an end, rather than an end in itself, can help you make sound investing decisions that align with your long-term objectives.

In addition to this, understanding the value of money is essential. This means appreciating the effort and time it takes to earn money and being conscious of how you choose to use and invest it. By valuing money and being mindful of your spending and investing habits, you can make more deliberate and informed decisions with your finances.

Embracing a Growth Mindset

A growth mindset is an essential component of a successful investing mindset. This mindset is about embracing challenges, persisting in the face of setbacks, and seeing failure as an opportunity to learn and grow. When it comes to investing, this mindset allows you to approach market fluctuations, investment performance, and financial setbacks as opportunities for learning and improvement.

By adopting a growth mindset, you can also become more open to new information and strategies, leading to continuous education and improvement in your investment approach. This mindset enables you to adapt to changes in the financial landscape and make necessary adjustments to your investment portfolio as needed.

Developing Patience and Discipline

Patience and discipline are crucial traits of successful investors. Patience allows you to take a long-term view of your investments and withstand short-term market volatility without making rash decisions. It involves understanding that building wealth takes time and that achieving your financial goals is a marathon, not a sprint.

Discipline, on the other hand, involves sticking to your investment strategy, even when faced with tempting short-term opportunities or fear-inducing market downturns. It's about staying the course and not allowing emotions to dictate your investment decisions. With patience and discipline, you can avoid impulsive actions that could derail your long-term financial success.

Fostering a Positive Relationship with Risk

A healthy investing mindset involves fostering a positive relationship with risk. While investing inherently involves risk, viewing it as a potential opportunity rather than a threat can help you make informed decisions and take calculated risks that align with your financial objectives. Understanding your risk tolerance and being comfortable with the level of risk in your investment portfolio is essential for maintaining a balanced and well-managed approach to investing.

Embracing risk also means recognizing that not all investments will pan out as expected, and that's okay. Learning to manage and mitigate risk through diversification, thorough research, and disciplined decision-making can enable you to navigate the uncertainties of the market with confidence.

Cultivating an Abundance Mindset

An abundance mindset is rooted in the belief that there are ample opportunities for financial growth and success. This mindset involves approaching investing with optimism, seeking out opportunities, and believing that your financial goals are attainable. By cultivating an abundance mindset, you can shift your focus from scarcity and limitation to abundance and opportunity, leading to a more proactive and optimistic approach to investing.

This mindset also encourages gratitude for the resources and opportunities available to you, which can positively impact your decision-making and overall financial well-being. It allows you to approach investing with a sense of abundance rather than fear, scarcity, or a constant need to chase returns.

Seeking Knowledge and Continuous Improvement

A successful investing mindset is never stagnant. It involves seeking out knowledge, staying informed about the latest market trends, and being open to new investment strategies and opportunities. Continuous improvement in your investing knowledge and skills is crucial for adapting to changes in the market and making informed decisions that align with your financial goals.

By embracing a commitment to ongoing learning and improvement, you can stay ahead of market developments, identify new investment opportunities, and refine your investment approach over time. This involves staying curious, reading widely, and seeking out mentors or professionals who can provide valuable insights and guidance.

Visualizing and Manifesting Financial Goals

Visualizing and manifesting your financial goals is a powerful aspect of a successful investing mindset. By clearly defining your financial objectives and creating a vision of what you want to achieve, you can channel your energy and focus toward making them a reality. This involves setting specific, measurable, achievable, relevant, and time-bound (SMART) goals that align with your long-term financial vision.

Visualizing your financial success can also help reinforce your commitment to your investment strategy and keep you motivated during challenging times. By visualizing the achievement of your financial goals, you can maintain a clear sense of purpose and direction in your investment journey.

Cultivating an Ethical and Responsible Approach

An essential aspect of a successful investing mindset involves cultivating an ethical and responsible approach to investing. This means making investment decisions that align with your values and beliefs, as well as considering the environmental, social, and governance (ESG) factors associated with your investments. By prioritizing ethical and responsible investing, you can contribute to positive social and environmental outcomes while also achieving your financial goals.

This approach involves conducting thorough due diligence on potential investments, considering the impact of your investment decisions beyond financial returns, and seeking out investment opportunities that align with your ethical principles. By integrating ethical considerations into your investment approach, you can invest with a clear conscience and contribute to a more sustainable and socially responsible financial ecosystem.

In conclusion, cultivating a successful investing mindset involves valuing money as a tool for achieving your goals, embracing a growth mindset, developing patience and discipline, fostering a positive relationship with risk, cultivating an abundance mindset, seeking knowledge and continuous improvement, visualizing and manifesting financial goals, and promoting an ethical and responsible approach to investing. By developing these key aspects of a successful investing mindset, you can enhance your financial journey and work toward building long-term wealth and financial security.

Modalities regarding money

When it comes to investing, it's important to understand the different modalities and options available for putting your money to work. There are several ways to invest money, each with its own characteristics and considerations. Here are some common modalities for investing money:

1. Stocks: Investing in stocks means buying ownership stakes in publicly traded companies. When you invest in stocks, you become a shareholder and have the potential to earn returns through stock price appreciation and dividends. Stocks can offer high potential returns, but they also come with a higher level of risk. It's important to research and analyze companies before investing in their stocks, and consider factors such as industry trends, financial performance, and management quality.

2. Bonds: Bonds are debt securities issued by governments, municipalities, or corporations to raise capital. When you invest in bonds, you are essentially lending money to the issuer in exchange for periodic interest payments and the return of the principal amount at the bond's maturity. Bonds are generally considered to be

lower risk than stocks, and they can provide a steady stream of income. However, bond prices can fluctuate based on changes in interest rates, so it's important to consider the interest rate environment when investing in bonds.

3. Mutual Funds: Mutual funds pool money from multiple investors to invest in a diversified portfolio of stocks, bonds, or other securities. By investing in a mutual fund, you can gain exposure to a wide range of assets without having to select and manage individual investments yourself. Mutual funds are managed by professional fund managers who make investment decisions on behalf of the fund's investors. They offer diversification and professional management, but they also come with fees and expenses that can impact overall returns.

4. Exchange-Traded Funds (ETFs): ETFs are similar to mutual funds in that they offer investors a way to gain exposure to a diversified portfolio of assets. However, ETFs trade on stock exchanges like individual stocks, and their prices can fluctuate throughout the trading day. ETFs may offer lower expense ratios compared to mutual funds, and they can be bought and sold throughout the trading day at market prices. Like mutual funds, ETFs can provide diversification and professional management, but it's important to consider trading costs and liquidity when investing in them.

5. Real Estate: Real estate investing involves buying, owning, and managing properties for the purpose of generating income and/or appreciation. Real estate can provide a steady stream of rental income and potential capital appreciation over time. There are various ways to invest in real estate, including direct ownership of properties, real estate investment trusts (REITs), real estate crowdfunding, and real estate partnerships. Real estate investing can offer diversification and a hedge against inflation, but it also comes with unique challenges such as property management and market volatility.

6. Retirement Accounts: Retirement accounts such as 401(k)s, IRAs, and Roth IRAs offer tax-advantaged ways to invest for retirement. These accounts allow individuals to invest in stocks, bonds, mutual funds, and other assets while enjoying tax benefits such as tax-deferred growth or tax-free withdrawals in retirement. Retirement accounts can be a powerful tool for long-term investing and wealth accumulation, and they offer a range of investment options based on individual risk tolerance and investment goals.

7. Alternative Investments: Alternative investments encompass a wide range of non-traditional assets such as private equity, hedge funds, commodities, cryptocurrency, and collectibles. These investments often have low correlation to traditional stocks and bonds, and they may offer the potential for higher returns and portfolio diversification. However, alternative investments can also come with higher fees, illiquidity, and regulatory complexities that require careful consideration and due diligence.

It's important to consider your investment goals, risk tolerance, time horizon, and financial situation when selecting investment modalities. Diversification across different asset classes and investment vehicles can help manage risk and optimize returns over the long term. Additionally, understanding the characteristics and risks of each modality can help you make informed investment decisions and build a well-structured investment portfolio.

When investing, it's also important to consider the impact of fees and expenses on investment returns. Different investment modalities come with varying costs, such as management fees, expense ratios, commissions, and transaction costs. These costs can erode investment returns over time, so it's essential to compare and evaluate the total costs associated with different investment options and consider how they may impact overall performance.

Furthermore, staying informed about market trends, economic indicators, and global events can help investors make well-informed decisions and adjust their investment strategies as needed. Regularly reviewing and rebalancing your investment portfolio can help ensure that it remains aligned with your investment objectives and risk tolerance.

In conclusion, investing money involves understanding and selecting from various modalities such as stocks, bonds, mutual funds, ETFs, real estate, retirement accounts, and alternative investments. Each modality has its own characteristics, risks, and potential rewards, and it's important to consider factors such as diversification, fees, and market dynamics when constructing an investment portfolio. By carefully evaluating different investment options and staying informed about market developments, investors can build a well-structured investment strategy that aligns with their financial goals and risk tolerance.

Managing expectations about money

We want success immediately and if we don't see the grass sprouting rapidly enough, we panic and may throw in the towel. The technology of the 21st century has enabled us to live in an instantaneous world.

Many of us, having taken advantage of all that the digital revolution has to offer, rely on instantaneous responses to set up and run our businesses. We are led to believe that this is the only path ahead and the only measure of success.

At the very least, we ask why, if we are doing all the right things, we are not experiencing results immediately, even though a few short weeks or months ago we willingly began despite knowing that short-term success is evaluated differently.

HAVE YOU MET MONEY?

My mom mentioned the other day that in her mother's day, it took up to six weeks for an international letter to arrive by boat and that was how it was. You anticipated nothing more.

I wonder how long entrepreneurs of the past had to wait for supplies or communications; their expectations would have had different parameters but they would still have had them and were required to manage them accordingly.

Please do not make this error, readers! In regulating your expectations, you will also be managing your success. I am speaking from experience, having fallen into the trap I just described.

A long time ago, I launched a new business in an area I understood little about, although having many transferable skills.

The new business offered great promise for me, my family and my future. So I set to work, completing all the various phases and stages, working through a plan (which had been given to me by a mentor) and at first I felt quite delighted with myself.

I didn't anticipate doing anything more than what I was doing at the time, which was working hard every day to establish the foundations for future success, as I mentioned previously. Approximately three weeks later, I panicked.

"I'm doing everything I can but no one is signing up for my list" (well, that's because it's a start-up and you need to get your brand out there; just because you're online doesn't mean that people will flock to you in droves before verifying that you are legit, trustworthy and here to stay, does it?) (I was still learning my art for the first three weeks, so I wasn't completely proficient!) Then I regained composure and reasoned with myself; everything made sense again.

The following week, it was "but I have these excellent things and many people are viewing my website, so why is no one purchasing anything?" Why wouldn't I expect my prospective customers to do the same? I do it myself: I visit a website that has piqued my attention, then I think about it, go back, take another look, and reconsider.

They will purchase, either on a first or subsequent visit and some will visit only once, comprehend the entire thing, find what they are looking for and click "Buy Now" there and without further consideration and they have done so but it's easy to fall into the wrong frame of mind when you are sleep deprived and exhausted from giving your all to your new concern.

Believe it or not, I fell into the same trap once more until I finally realized what I was doing and changed my thinking so that I would be prepared the next time similar doubts arrived on the horizon.

Once I had made those all-important and incredibly thrilling initial sales, there was a brief gap until the next one and before I knew it, I wondered, "Why hasn't anyone purchased anything this week?"

I realized at this time that I couldn't continue in this manner if I was in it for a long haul and that a year or so later, I would likely laugh at my flimsy resolve and at how easily I was momentarily derailed by impatient doubt. I am an expert on this subject - it was one of my transferable abilities!

I was also fortunate that I had a mentor (you will hear me mention this a lot - I do not believe you can underestimate the value of having someone to turn to with the experience you are still acquiring) who reminded me how well things were going for such a young business and that rather than bemoaning my apparent slow progress, I should be proud of everything that has gone well.

We view our shortcomings rather than our strengths almost as a default position. Manage your expectations. Set them realistically at the outset, write goals down if necessary and always evaluate your progress about them.

Just make sure you don't move the goal posts unless it's for a good business purpose and you were planning to adjust them once you saw how things were going.

In the first phases or while introducing a new initiative or product that may need time to establish itself, do not allow pessimism to overtake your desired measured perspective.

You will achieve success exactly as planned by keeping your head in the game and by adjusting your expectations properly, you will also discover the pleasure of managing your success.

Understanding the risks of money

It appears that everyone is eager to understand how to get wealthy. There are thousands of books written specifically on how to become wealthy.
Also, hundreds of classes and seminars on how to become wealthy are regularly held in various parts of the world. However, despite the abundance of available resources, there appear to be only a few success stories.

How do you become wealthy if millions of people have failed before you? You must begin with the proper mindset for producing money.

What exactly is the psychology of making money? The psychology of making money entails the behavior and mental processes involved in generating income. We must comprehend how our thoughts and emotions influence our behavior.

There are many ways to make money, including starting a business, writing books, creating a website, etc. However, if you lack the proper mentality for making money, you'll wipe out your savings and lose more money than you would make.

Among the most common mistakes made by individuals is to believe that wealth provides instant gratification. To become wealthy, you must act like the wealthy.

I don't suggest spending money on flashy cars, the newest gadgets or designer clothes; rather, imitate the wealthy by taking calculated risks, making strategic investments and saving money for the future.

Every one of us is capable of earning a living. However, it might be very tough for most people to make it expand. So how does one become wealthy without stealing from banks? You must be cautious with your financial decisions.

When experiencing tremendous happiness, anger, sadness or any other emotion, you can wish to delay making a decision. Our actions are most susceptible when we are in an emotionally unstable state.

Many researches indicate that depressed individuals tend to spend more money unintentionally. To escape this despair, people typically spend money on a few drinks or extravagant vacation.

This demonstrates the effect of our emotions on how we handle money. How can one become wealthy if they work long hours but spend their money instantly whenever they feel down?

Not forgetting that a lack of money can also lead to depression, which contributes to emotionally-driven purchasing cycles.

Prepare yourself and adopt the proper mindset for producing money. Never let opportunities pass you by and always be up for a challenge.

There are a thousand different ways to discover how to become wealthy. If you follow the history of how wealthy people became wealthy, you will find that there is no single secret method.

As vital as learning how to become wealthy is, **it is more crucial to know what to do with the money you already have**, rather than relying on future earnings. To become wealthy, you must also take <u>**measured risks, make strategic investments, and always save for the future to remain wealthy**</u>.

One man's debt are another man's assets

Your biggest asset is your earning capacity and your greatest resource is your time, according to a quote attributed to American television host Brian Tracy; if this adage is accurate, it implies that we all can increase our net worth (by compounding our assets and annihilate our liabilities) but what are these assets and liabilities from a financial standpoint? How do they contribute to an individual's net worth?

If you apply for an unsecured loan from a reputable lender, they will ask you a series of personal questions to determine your creditworthiness, i.e., your ability to repay the loan, by examining your income and expenses and determining whether you have a deficit or surplus. If you ask for a secured loan, the lender will evaluate your creditworthiness and net worth by determining your assets and liabilities.

An asset is anything possessed by a person (or organization) that can (potentially) generate revenue; in other words, it is anything with an economic worth that can be converted to cash, such as a car, property,' skills,' cash, securities, bonds, etc.

In contrast, liability depletes a person's funds, such as a loan, mortgage, shop cards, credit cards, etc. Liability is also described as the obligation of a person (or entity) to repay a debt.

Most people consider their mortgaged homes (primary domicile property) an asset. Strictly speaking, it is only an asset to the bank short term but in the long run (assuming that the property worth would improve over time; as we've all seen during the recent recession, house values have fallen into negative equity, with the purchase price exceeding the current market value).

The house you reside in (and the automobile you drive) are liabilities in the near term, as they reduce your income without providing any returns for you.

Thus, a person's net worth is calculated by subtracting their assets from their liabilities; if all their assets are sold and the returns are used to pay off their liabilities (debts, commitments), the difference is their net worth. This indicates that negative net worth is feasible, i.e., when the total value of assets is less than the entire value of obligations.

Bill Gates, whose estimated net worth is the US $22bn, has reclaimed his position as the world's richest man, surpassing Warren Buffet, whose estimated net worth is the US $12bn (both damaged by the current recession; Gates lost $18bn and Buffet lost $25bn).

These two billionaires' net worth declined significantly due to a decline in their assets. Increasing one's obligations is a second method for lowering one's net worth.

None of the twelve adults I know socially recognized their net worth and only three of the twelve (25%) knew what net worth was and how it is calculated from one's financial data (information).

This is unfortunate because a person's net worth is the greatest financial leverage (muscle) one may own and utilize in the financial arena.

On a non-financial level, I believe it is important to note that some objects and people are assets while others are liabilities. People (family, friends, acquaintances), abilities, expertise, etc. that enable you to be and do more in life are "rare and valuable" to

you. To achieve greatness in life, you need to identify and eliminate those relationships and personal behaviors that are a liability.

Most people believe that asset protection is only necessary for those with a net worth over many million dollars. They may consider Swiss bank accounts and tax havens and conclude that protection is not for them because they are working class or middle class. ***This is false!***

Regardless of the precise value of your assets, it is essential to safeguard them. Homeowners must ensure their home's equity, especially if they do not reside in a state that automatically exempts homes from creditors.

If you own a vehicle or have invested in valuables such as artwork, diamonds, and jewelry, you must ensure its security. Again, this is not only about enormous wealth. An engagement ring is an investment in jewelry and inheriting jewelry or art means you now possess these assets.

In addition, you may have investments in savings accounts, equities and bonds, all of which could be in danger if you are found liable in a court settlement or are attacked by creditors. A bankruptcy attorney will assist you in developing a solid protection plan in many situations.
Typically, bankruptcy attorneys know how creditors operate and what will be at risk if you fail to preserve your assets. Discuss your alternatives for protection and the consequences of forgoing protection with an expert.

While some may be startled by the legality of offshore investing opportunities, others recognize that this is among the best ways to safeguard your assets. There are many methods for utilizing offshore protection measures.

Creditors will have easy trouble locating your offshore accounts but any U.S. court order regarding these assets will be invalid. The assets are governed by the laws and regulations of the nation in which they are invested.

The only way for the creditors to access these assets would be if they traveled to that nation, had their case adjudicated in that country's courts and achieved a settlement equal to what they were seeking in the United States. It is doubtful that a creditor will commit the necessary time and resources to achieve this.

Transferring your possessions to someone else is a second alternative for asset protection, sometimes known as the poor man's asset protection.

This is a potentially unsafe action even when transferring to a trusted family member. If the relationship fails, you will be out of luck.

Your adversary now owns all of your property, which will be upheld in court. There is also the possibility that the creditors will prove the transfer was fraudulent.

This indicates that the court believes you shifted these assets to avoid paying your debt. This is not illegal but the court can simply disregard or reverse the transfer, putting you back where you started. To avoid being accused of fraudulent transfer, make asset protection decisions well in advance of implementing a protection strategy.
Look into **_anonymity compliant business structure_**.

Make SMART goals

Regardless of your desired outcome, you must have structure to keep you moving forward properly.

HAVE YOU MET MONEY?

The acronym SMART stands for the five criteria used to establish goals.

• Specific: When goals are specific, it is clear what is anticipated, when and in what quantity. Because the goals are specific, monitoring your progress towards achieving them is simple.

• Measurable: It is easy to remain motivated to fulfill your goals when there are milestones that reflect their progression. What use is a goal that cannot be measured? If your objectives are not measurable, you will never know if you are making progress toward achieving them.

• Attainable: When goals are set too high or too low, they become meaningless and you grow upset, lose focus or neglect them altogether. Goals should be neither too easy nor unattainable.

• Relevant: A goal is realistic if you have the resources to achieve it. Realistic objectives need resources such as people, equipment, money, talents, etc. to be attained.

• Time-bound: Goals should include a start date, an end date and intermediate benchmarks. Setting a deadline is essential for maintaining momentum. Without deadlines or completion timelines, goals can be derailed by life's daily drama.

Improving one's physical fitness is a good example of a circumstance that needs SMART goals. You must define the who, what, when, where and how and why.

Specific:

- Who: Only you

- What: Drop 30 pounds

- What: six months

- required at home and the gym

- Why: per doctor's advice and to become in better condition

- How: exercise three times per week for two hours

Measurable: Check your progress every week to ensure you're on track. This also helps you maintain your motivation.

Attainable: Can you lose 30lbs in 6 months? That would equate to 5 pounds per month. Considering your weekly development, is this a realistic goal?

Relevant: Do you have enough time to make the objectives attainable?

Do you have the means to exercise at home? Will the gym be affordable?

Milestones at defined intervals mean that you must drop at least 5 pounds every month. Will your timeline consist of weekly scale weigh-ins?

The key to SMART is to remember that it's your life. Therefore, cautious planning will keep you on track to achieve your goals promptly. What should you have accomplished in six months, one year, three years, five years, and ten years?

Once you have discovered what you want to do with your life, you can set some goals. Start with your short-term goals, such as daily, weekly and monthly objectives, which will help you achieve your long-term goals.

Everyone has dreams. Using SMART objectives, can you achieve your dreams? Possibly, you are establishing objectives without a defined procedure. Inspiration to pursue intelligent objectives is the initial step. As you achieve your objectives, your drive and inspiration should grow. Yes!

Financial Responsibility

Financial matters, credit ratings, debt management, and bankruptcy are frequently discussed in today's society. Therefore, it is ethical to believe that the global community must become more financially responsible.

What precisely does being financially responsible entail?

It might have varied meanings for many individuals based on their requirements and financial status. Regardless of your age or present financial situation, it is never too late to become financially responsible.

Financial responsibility does not come naturally; people must alter how they think about and use money. You should gain much knowledge as possible regarding debt, credit and credit scores to comprehend how your actions may affect your future.

If you have a significant other with whom you share accounts, you must ensure that you both commit to becoming more responsible.

After analyzing your debt and credit ratings or credit history, you should build a budget. If you are not sure of how to accomplish this, examine your last month's bills; if you don't have any, estimate or contact an electric or cable company to obtain an estimated average monthly statement.
These expenses represent your outcome, so you must now examine your income. If you already have problems with spending more than you earn, examine your bills to determine where you can save money; you cannot need all those High-Definition and movie channels. '

After determining how much of your income is spent on bills, you must examine your other expenses, such as petrol, food and entertainment. If you feel these additional expenses are straining your finances, you can reduce them.

People appear to take savings accounts for granted. They are offered by banks so that you can, well, save. After reviewing your monthly bills, other expenses and income, you should consider how much you can set aside for savings. They recommend having at least six months' worth of salary in an emergency fund in case you lose your job.

On average, it takes six months to find new work. Depending on your luck, it may take less time but you should set aside money just in case.

Avoid depleting your savings account. Use your savings as an emergency fund because you never know when you'll have a flat tire, a medical emergency or a car accident. Having an emergency fund provides a little buffer for unforeseen circumstances. You can also use the earnings to make a down payment on a home or car or to take a trip.

After analyzing your savings, income and expenses, you must build a budget for yourself and your family. This varies from person to person; you can not wish to save six months' worth of money or desire all of those premium channels. The most important thing is to be aware of your spending habits so that you can alter them if necessary.

If you need assistance with organization, you might consult a financial advisor to see if they can assist you. Managing your finances well can prevent you from incurring debt and possibly help you achieve and/or maintain a high credit score.

HAVE YOU MET MONEY?

If individuals saved more and spent less, they would incur less debt and enjoy greater financial independence. Debt is not simply a personal problem.

It imposes a financial strain on the debtor's family, peers and society. In the end, it is our tax dollars that assist people in serious debt to file for bankruptcy.

It is tough to exercise self-control in a society where people are continually pressured to purchase luxury products they cannot afford or do not need.

You can encounter extreme financial circumstances. Perhaps you are attempting to eliminate debt while meeting your monthly financial responsibilities.'
'
Taking financial responsibility starts with one basic step: recording expenses. You must detail all of your expenses for an entire month. Include even modest expenses such as morning coffee and the newspaper purchase in the afternoon.
Create three categories for your expenses: fixed, variable and luxury. Fixed expenses are expenses, such as utility payments, are the same each month.

Variable expenses include medical and periodic insurance premiums. Expenses categorized as luxuries are those that can be done without.

Understanding the distinction between a want and a need is the first step in becoming financially responsible. A need is something you should have to survive, such as food, whereas a want is something you simply desire, such as new shoes.

Avoid marketing messages that create the illusion of affluence but result in debt. The purchase of new vehicles or holidays is not profitable investments. Cars never appreciate.

Consequently, a new automobile is a poor investment. Focus on long-term, steady assets that will appreciate over some years if you wish to assume financial responsibility.

Learning to save and having the self-discipline to begin saving immediately is also a terrific skill for assuming financial responsibility.

Put away any extra money you can afford at the end of the month. Create a six-month emergency fund if you lose your job or become very ill.

Your financial issues can quickly become a family burden and a societal issue. Now is the time to assume financial responsibility by managing debt, saving for the future and generating income through intelligent and dependable investments.

Chapter Two:
What is Money?

Currency

A currency Is the standardization of money in any form, including banknotes and coins, in use or circulation as a medium of exchange.

A currency is a system of money commonly used within a given setting over time, particularly by citizens of a country state. According to Wikipedia, money is a means of commerce, a unit of account and a store of value.

The first category of this concept applies to currency, which is merely one kind of money. Currency is also the lowest component of economists' "money supply". The money supply consists of various components, including credit, deposit accounts, etc.

Since the vast majority of e-currencies are employed as units of value in exchange for goods and services, the vast majority qualify as money and currency.

Moreover, I believe that Visa(tm) and MasterCard(tm) dollar units are also currencies, despite the companies' wishes to the contrary (this view may be controversial to some).

Credit card accounts are the most prevalent e-currencies in circulation today. In today's technological environment, the gap between traditional and e-currency is nonexistent.

The distinction between government-issued (or "public") currencies and those issued by private corporations is the most intriguing (call them "private").

With the advent and widespread use of PayPal, private (e-)currencies became an overnight trending issue. PayPal was among the first private currencies unaffiliated with governments or credit card companies. However, private currencies are not novel.

The original currency in the United States consisted of privately produced "Bank Notes" issued by banks in the United States. In the early days of this country, they played a crucial function since they had value regardless of whether the United States continued to exist as an independent nation. You may view some of these fascinating documents in a coin shop.

Generally, the first US bank notes were backed by a precious metal; in reality, they were often gold or silver certificates that could be exchanged at the bank for the precious metal. A bank account was a gold cache for which certificates were issued.

Later, the US government produced its own money, which consisted of gold or silver certificates. In 1972, the United States "abandoned the gold standard," which linked the dollar's value to a set quantity of gold.

Before that period, the United States government was compelled to back the value of its currency with gold stored in depository facilities throughout the country. Although Fort Knox is the most recognizable of these installations, it is by no means the largest.

Fiat Currency

Rather than a tangible product or financial instrument, it is backed by the government of a country. This indicates that most coin and paper currencies used worldwide are fiat money.

The dollar, the pound, the rupee and the euro are included. The value of fiat money is largely determined by public confidence in the issuer.

The value of a fiat system, which consists of fiat money, is determined solely by government regulation or law. In such a society, money is an intrinsically worthless good, as any tangible physical product does not support it.

Fiat money, also known as fiat currency, may only be valuable if used to purchase products or pay taxes. Consequently, a system based on fiat currency tends toward a higher degree of insecurity, as its credibility is typically lost when the issuing government refuses to guarantee its worth through further taxation.

One of the biggest disadvantages of a fiat monetary system is that there are no limits on the amount of money issued. Consequently, economies can increase their money supply following population needs, which, over the long run, results in economic devaluation and ultimately financial catastrophe.
Within a fiat monetary system, the value of money is dependent mostly on confidence. Once that trust is no longer present, the "Tinkerbell effect" also evaporates. This implies that the value of money disappears, leaving behind nothing but dismay.

With most global economies utilizing fiat currencies, the prospect of hyperinflation has never been more imminent. Governments that have experienced fiat money inflation have exerted enormous effort to construct a functional and stable economic framework.

However, gold has always passed the durability test in the rather volatile fiat monetary system and is usually regarded as a safe investment.

Gold's growing value over time makes it an excellent hedge against fiat money inflation. This is feasible since gold prices will likely skyrocket when the value of fiat currency falls.

If you decide to purchase this precious metal as a kind of insurance against fiat currency crises or just to diversify your portfolio of assets, adhere to the advice of financial experts and choose mostly actual gold. Also, before making a purchase, remember to visit the stores of multiple vendors. This will guarantee you the lowest price.

In countries whose economies are built on a fiat system, fiat currency is regularly encountered. Any tangible commodity does not back fiat currency. Its worth is mostly determined by government regulation or law. The usage of fiat currency for purchasing things and paying taxes is prevalent. However, any fiat monetary system has a propensity to be quite insecure.

In a fiat monetary system, there are no limits on the issuance of currency. As a result, an inexhaustible amount of credit is generated.

Most people first view a rapid expansion of credit availability as an indicator of economic growth. However, in the long run, such a trend leads to economic depreciation and financial collapse.

Hyperinflation poses an impending threat to governments that utilize fiat currencies. When hyperinflation develops, money loses its credibility and becomes worthless since it can no longer be utilized as a medium of exchange. Since most large economies are dependent on fiat currencies, the likelihood of hyperinflation is extremely high.

Moreover, efforts to recover from fiat currency hyperinflation are extremely difficult. Most administrations that have experienced such a crisis have had to systematically rebuild a stable economic climate.

Investing in gold is recommended if you wish to prevent this circumstance. This precious metal is commonly viewed as a hedge against severe financial collapse, as its price tends to rise dramatically when the value of fiat currency falls.

There are many strategies for investing in gold. Among the most prevalent is the purchase of gold bullion bars. Bullion gold bars are available in various sizes. Also, you may easily resell them at the counter of the big banks, sometimes tax-free.

Gold sovereigns represent an additional opportunity to boost the portfolio's worth. This piece, made of 22-karat gold, was first minted during the reign of King Henry the Seventh of England.

This one-of-a-kind piece of gold will provide financial stability and a sense of having acquired a piece of British historical heritage.

Hard money

Originally, "hard money" referred to the physical properties of metallic currency, which, in contrast to paper currency, is formed of hard substances. This originates from the English expression " hard, cold cash."

The distinction between "soft" paper currency and "hard" metal coins derives from the fact that metal coins are actual, physical units with intrinsic economic value regardless of their monetary status. In contrast, fiat currency issued on paper is nothing other than a promise to pay the holder in actual currency upon redemption.

In the absence of metallic currencies, hard money often refers to a variety of monetary instruments that, in domestic and international markets, operate more similarly to metallic currencies.
It is believed that this currency will retain a stable value relative to goods and a solid exchange rate relative to weaker currencies. Hard money has been historically regarded for its vastly superior use as a medium of commerce, store accounting device and value.

Today, most nations issue "soft" or fiat money, which is not backed by any tangible object. In addition, the term hard money has other meanings related to a person's or an object's dependability or confidence.

Hard money maintains a constant market value relative to tangible goods and a strong exchange rate relative to foreign currencies.

Hard money serves the economic purposes of money (as a store of value, a medium of exchange and a unit of account) more successfully than softer monies, whose value fluctuates more.

The transaction costs and risks associated with hard cash are lower than those associated with soft currency. This distinction began with comparing the confidence in the metallic standard of commodity money and metallic content and it has since been applied to different modern paper or fiat currencies.

There is a correlation between "hard" versus "soft" money and the relative stability of exchange rates since the value of paper currencies fluctuates on the foreign exchange market based on faith in the payment commitments they represent and depreciates over time when issuers inflate their supply.

This means that hard currency has a better exchange rate than soft currency since it is more stable regarding real goods and services over time.

HAVE YOU MET MONEY?

A currency is only useful for trade and a store of value if it is accepted as a unit of account by the general population.

Because of its constant value, hard money has long been the favored medium of trade, store of value, and unit of account for profit and loss accounting.

Gresham's Law was born out of this predisposition (the other part being legal tender laws). Having a currency with less volatility or a currency that loses value over time reduces the usefulness of soft money.

This contrast between hard and soft paper currencies was maintained as governments steadily abandoned the use and legal tender status of precious metal backing and precious metal money such as the gold standard in favor of paper currency.

In today's world, "hard money" is typically used to refer to fiat currency issued by a stable and conservative government that restricts the issuance of cash.

Over time, these currencies have a more stable exchange rate and a lower rate of inflation-induced depreciation. Some of the world's most developed countries, such as Switzerland, place a high value on maintaining a hard currency policy. Because of this, hard currency is in great demand on the international market for use as a bank reserve in international trade settlements.

Those who adhere to the Austrian economics theory, such as Libertarians, believe restoring hard money is necessary to achieve economic stability.

Various Synonyms for "Hard Money"

In a variety of financial situations, hard currency is also utilized. These words are associated with the fundamental economic dichotomy between hard and soft currency. They demonstrate the confidence or reliability parties can place in specific money or financing.

A hard currency consist of coins minted from precious metals and minerals, such as platinum, silver and gold. This product has become popular on the market but many people are still unsure what hard money is. Hard money is non-conventional or private financing with private funds, as defined by me.

Bullion

Bullion is defined as the bulk of any of the available precious metals. Precious metals are metallic elements that are regarded as uncommon.

The value of bullion, which is often composed of gold or silver, is determined by the value of the metal, not the face value. The mass and purity of the metal, not a fictitious face value, determine the value of bullion.

While advancements have been made to the mining and processing precious metals, new mineral sources have also been discovered.

Based on these two criteria, the value of gold, silver and other precious metals may decline. The market value or amount of demand determines how precious metals are classified.

Bullion is traded on commodities exchanges in the form of ingots or coins. A nation's government mints its coins. The face values of legal tender bullion coins are far less than the actual commodity worth of the metals. At the time of minting, face values are assigned to bullion coins.

HAVE YOU MET MONEY?

For instance, the vast majority of gold coins minted by national governments with monetary values between 10 and 100 US dollars contain at least 31 grams of gold.

Considering the constant increase in the price of gold per ounce, the value of a gram of gold is around 12 US dollars. Government-assigned value of the gold bullion coin has no significance.

Australian Gold nuggets worth $10,000 are one of the largest bullion coins. This Australian government-minted bullion coin contains 1 kilogram of 99.9 percent pure gold. The Australian Gold Nugget is not the largest gold coin a national government has ever struck.
The larger coins are not mass-produced and are difficult to manipulate. Among the government-issued gold and silver bullion coins are the following:

1. China's Golden Panda

2. Austrian Philharmoniker

3. American Buffalo, American Eagle and

4. Australian Gold Nugget

5. Mexican Centenario, Onza and Libertand

6. Polish Orzel Bielik

7. Krugerrand, South Africa

8. Swiss Vreneli

9. British Britannia and Sovereign

10. Canadian Maple Leaf

Metal, purity and weight are the three determinants of bullion's worth. The metal used to create each bullion coin is the primary determinant.

Silver is the least valued precious metal, with gold immediately preceding it and platinum being the most valuable. Silver coins are currently more popular among collectors due to their affordability.

Bars

What is a gold bar?

These are refined metallic gold in any form produced by a bar manufacturer who adheres to established manufacturing, labeling and documentation requirements. Ingots, manufactured by pouring molten metal into a mold, are larger than smaller bars, created by stamping gold sheets.

Central Bank gold reserves are standard gold bars exchanged by a bullion dealer and weigh approximately 12.4 kilograms or 438.9 ounces.

A kilo bar containing one thousand grams is widely used in trade and investment and is typically flat. However, some investors prefer the brick shape.

What types of bars exist?

Although there are more than 30 types of gold bars in circulation on the global gold market today, it is primarily divided into two categories based on production: cast and minted.

Casting involves pouring molten gold into an ingot mold, whereas minting involves hand-cutting gold blanks or flat pieces of gold to the desired dimensions. Typically, the markings on bars are applied via pressing.

The Chip Gold is a new type of bar consisting of a miniature ingot containing between 1 and 20 grams of gold. They are sealed and certified and are about the size of a credit card.

What is the standard weight of its bars?

Gold bars are measured in troy ounces, where one troy equals 31.1034768 grams. In countries that utilize imperial measures, however, the avoirdupois ounce is used to measure weight. The Avoirdupois ounce weighs less than the troy ounce, which equals 28.349523125 grams.

However, bars held by central banks that are internationally traded and regarded as standards are also known as Good Delivery bars and typically weigh around 400 ounces.

However, the amount of gold fluctuates between 350 and 450 ounces, with a minimum purity standard of 99.5%. These bars are held in recognized and safe bullion vaults to preserve their quality.

Rounds

In some form, round cuts have existed since at least the seventeenth century. "round brilliant" refers to a particular kind of diamond cutting that produces the most uniform brilliance and reflection. Whereas previous round cuts, such as the cushion cut, typically had fewer facets.

Fewer facets resulted in longer facets and as longer facets disclose faults inside the diamond, these early varieties of round cuts were only suitable for extremely rare, perfect diamonds.

In contrast, the round has a greater number of tiny facets. This allows the cut to conceal some flaws that may exist within a diamond. In the end, the round has significantly increased the availability of beautiful gems.

The perfect round cut is believed to contain between 56 and 60 facets, even though the opinions of various gemologists vary significantly. If a diamond has an extremely high number of faults or inclusions, it is feasible to manufacture additional facets when necessary.

Round brilliant diamonds' benefits

The fundamental benefit of round diamonds and their immense appeal is their ability to conceal defects. With other diamond shapes, diamonds with clarity classifications of SI1 or SI2 may have inclusions that are apparent to the human eye. Still, with rounds, imperfections can be concealed even within this range.

In addition, the brilliant round cut does an excellent job of accentuating the diamond's innate reflectivity and brilliance. The unusual brilliance that diamonds emit is one of their most alluring qualities and the round brilliant is one of the best cuts for maximizing this natural characteristic.

The durability of round diamonds is an additional benefit. The corners and sides of shapes with straight edges, such as the emerald cut, are susceptible to harm, whereas the round shape of diamonds naturally protects them from damage.

Selecting the most desirable round brilliant diamonds

While some other diamond shapes have potential design flaws that might cause aesthetic issues, round brilliants have a highly constant appearance; therefore, buyers can concentrate on the grades of a round brilliant to choose the greatest value.

With one important exception, the rules for getting the most value for your dollar with round diamonds are identical to those for other cuts. For the cut grade, "Very Good," "Good," or comparable evaluations indicate value.

The round brilliant's ability to conceal inclusions allows for a lower clarity rating than with other diamonds. Therefore, SI1 or SI2 will provide a fair value without sacrificing the look to the human eye. In the color section, search for something between G and I. Lastly, carat weight should be 1 or less, unless you intend to spend a lot.

Precious Metals

These are rare metals which have a high economic worth due to different characteristics, including their rarity, usage in industrial operations, protection against currency inflation and role as a store of value throughout history.
Gold, platinum and silver are the most popular precious metals among investors. There are eight precious metals in existence. Gold, rhodium, ruthenium, silver, platinum, palladium, iridium and osmium are among them.

Precious metals are uncommon chemical elements with a high and lasting monetary worth. They are less reactive than most elements and are distinguished by their brilliance and high melting points.

The most well-known metals are silver and gold, whose uses span from jewelry to coins to art and whose economic relevance has been acknowledged in recent years.

Platinum, essentially a byproduct, is today one of the most often traded precious metals, along with ruthenium, rhodium, palladium, osmium and iridium.

The nature of precious metals may be derived from the fact that they are extremely rare and distinctive among other commodities, which also accounts for their quality being deemed high monetary value and, therefore, a measure of wealth.

It is also essential to remember that not all precious metals retain their value permanently. This is contingent upon their availability and innovative refining or generating methods.

Aluminum, for example, was previously one of the most difficult metals to extract from its ore, despite being one of the most abundant. When a simple method of aluminum extraction was developed in the late 1800s, its once-exalted status plummeted substantially.

Variations in the rarity of metals are dependent on demand. Silver, for example, has a supply deficit since more silver is consumed than is mined. Therefore, it is expected to cost more than gold in the foreseeable future.

In addition to scarcity, other common properties of metals, such as applications, storage ease, similar origin and historical worth, are considered distinguishing traits for precious metals.

It is also difficult to refute precious metals' industrial applications, making them even more desirable. Finding new applications for them boosts their trade and commodities market worth.

Protecting your silver and/or gold precious metals from theft is the most crucial reason to acquire secure storage when purchasing precious metals.

Noble Metals

Noble metals are a collection of 17 metallic elements with comparable properties and structures that are indispensable in producing a growing number of high-tech applications.

They are essential components in high-tech devices such as smartphones and hybrid automobiles. They are also utilized in computer discs, guided missiles, television screens, microphones, photovoltaic cells, energy-efficient lighting and wind energy. The list is exhaustive.

The extensive application of these essential components explains their high demand. However, the supply chain is difficult for manufacturers of the type of items that rely so heavily on them.

This collection of elements is not very rare, despite its name. They are prevalent in many mineral deposits around the world. So why are they referred to as "rare," and why is the availability of these essential elements such a burden for the industry?

The fundamental issue is that noble metals are not found in economically viable concentrations in any one location. Typically extracted as a byproduct of other mining operations, they are widely dispersed around the earth. Consequently, their acquisition can be excessively expensive.

China has been the only nation to harvest rare earth materials in large amounts during the past decade. As a result, China has built a stranglehold over the market, controlling over 95% of global trade, including two most essential rare piles of earth, Dysprosium and Neodymium.

China has tightened export limits in response to surging local demand and ostensibly protected the environment by limiting mining operations, putting global firms and governments into a frenzy.

Different sources

Other nations have rare earth metal reserves but China has a significant edge because of its low-cost labor and lax environmental regulations. However, this reliance has prompted the hunt for alternative economically feasible sources.

According to the US Geological Survey, noble elements (REE) deposits in the United States include roughly 13 million metric tonnes. Molycorp now operates the largest mine in California. Avalon, a firm located in Canada and North America, is a second active business in the region.

The world is currently looking to Myanmar (Burma) as an alternative supply of this valuable commodity, among other locations.

The nation is renowned for its rare earth, including Xenotime, Monazite, Columbite and Tantalite. President Thein Sein's reforms have prompted tech-savvy and eager industrial behemoths to examine Myanmar's reserves.

Exploration of rare volcanic rocks in the harsh, dangerous deserts of southern Afghanistan has uncovered world-class concentrations of the desired components.

Geologists have mapped one million metric tons of these key elements, including lanthanum, cerium and neodymium, which could meet the world's needs for ten years based on current consumption levels.

The United States Geological Survey considers these figures to be conservative. Exploration has been severely restricted due to the location of the deposit in the most dangerous province in the country, Helmand; nonetheless, additional exploration may yield a huge discovery.

The concentration of so-called light rare earth elements in the Afghan deposit is comparable to that of the premier site mined in

China; hence, Afghanistan could serve as an alternate source for industrialized nations.

Due to security concerns and a lack of infrastructures such as trains to transport ore and an enlarged electrical grid to power machines, which would need to be created first, it seems unlikely that the about USD7.4 billion rich deposit will be mined soon.

Therefore, it is evident that China's virtual monopoly on the supply of noble metals will keep these vital minerals "rare" for the foreseeable future, raising their value as global industrial demand continues to climb. Consequently, investing in precious metals is a very tempting option.

U.S. Dollar index

The U.S. dollar index (USDX) measures the dollar's value relative to a basket of international currencies. The US Federal Reserve launched the USDX in 1973.

The symbol for the US Dollar Index is $DXY and is commonly known as the Dixie. Contracts for futures on the US Dollar Index are traded on the ICE Futures Exchange, previously the New York Board of Trade (NYBOT). You've probably noticed that this indicator is significantly weighted towards the EURO.

Before the introduction of the EURO, this index included the French Franc, the German Mark, the Italian Lira and other European currencies.

In 1999, when the EURO became the EMU's single currency, it replaced the abovementioned currencies. Therefore, there is a strong bias against this one currency.

Professional traders diversify their spot USD trades with USDX. As stated, the USDX is now significantly biased in favor of the EURO by more than 50 percent.

It is often used for trading EUR/USD. EUR/USD and USDX both move in opposite directions. When EUR/USD increases, USDX decreases. You must be aware of this reality.

You may have noticed that the US Dollar Index is highly skewed toward the EURO; more than fifty percent of the index's weight is attributed to this currency.

This indicates that this index can, to some extent, follow the market movement of the EURO currency. The EUR/USD pair follows the EUR. The US Dollar Index can be utilized while trading the EUR/USD pair. As stated previously, USDX and EUR/USD move in opposite directions.
Suppose you are engaged in EUR/USD trading on a daily chart! It is in an uptrend and is approaching a support area. You examine the USDX chart.

Since USDX and EUR/USD are moving in different directions, USDX should be in a decline and close to reaching a level of resistance. If this observation is confirmed on the USDX chart, you can open a long position in EUR/USD.

In the preceding example, USDX verified your EUR/USD trading signal. Assume that the EUR/USD chart indicates that price activity is poised to break out in a new direction. A head and shoulders chart pattern is built on the intraday EUR/USD chart.

The trend has risen! This indicates that a new trend in the direction of decline should be anticipated with high probability. When EUR/USD declines, the USD rises or the market is USD positive.

You investigate the USDX chart. It is also in an uptrend and on the verge of breaking out of a head and shoulders formation. This indicates a potential decline in the US Dollar Index. In other words, a USD depreciation or USD bears.

The EUR/USD chart currently provides a bullish USD forecast, whereas the USDX chart provides a negative USD outlook. These two signals do not confirm one another. Therefore, a short position in EUR/USD should be avoided.

The U.S. Dollar Index (USDX) is an indicator that provides an overview of the performance of the U.S. Dollar relative to a set of currencies.

It resembles the Dow Jones Industrial Average in many ways (DJIA). The DJIA is the average price of a group of equities that gives traders an indication of market performance.

The Euro (EUR), the Japanese Yen (JPY), the British Pound (GBP), the Canadian Dollar (CAD), the Swiss Franc (CHF) and the Swedish Krona (SEK) make up the U.S. Dollar index (SEK). By analyzing the performance of the U.S. dollar versus these foreign currencies, we can gauge the global strength of the American economy.

Mining

Mining is extracting rich minerals and other geological materials from the Earth, typically from an ore body, seam, lode, vein, reef or placer deposit.

In mines, extremely valuable and in-demand materials are harvested. These precious minerals consist of copper, coal, iron, lead and many other earth-derived geological components. Mines may be located underground, subsurface or on the surface. As long as an area of land may be viewed as one from which a mineral can be taken, it is termed a mine.

Many resources can be extracted from mining regions. Some minerals that can be extracted from mines are precious metals and basic metals in their ore form. Other substances, such as rock salt, uranium, coal, limestone, potash and diamond, can also be removed using mining methods.

As long as agricultural processes cannot create a material or if a material cannot be manufactured in factories or laboratories, these materials most likely originated from mines.

There are copper, coal, lead, and iron mines in operation today. Due to the high demand for these metals in the building industry, iron and copper mines are the main industry on a global scale. Coal mines are typically used to extract fuel and energy, while lead mines are utilized to meet the demand for stable heavy metals.

Other mines, such as diamond mines, exist for aesthetic purposes. Diamonds are a valuable product in the fashion and jewelry industries and as a precious mineral, they are highly costly. Many diamond mines are located in Africa, where the mining of diamonds has exacerbated certain conflicts.

Heavy machinery is required for mineral extraction. For land extraction, bulldozers, explosives, vehicles and drills are necessary. Trams convey the miners and the minerals, while lifts bring them into and out of the mines.

In surface mining, enormous trucks, shovels and cranes transport vast volumes of ore. You will find roasters, crushers, mills and reactors in processing plants. They aid in extracting metals, minerals and other essential substances from ores.

Minting

HAVE YOU MET MONEY?

A mint is a facility that produces coins for cash. In the United States, the US Government Mint is responsible for producing sufficient quantities of cash for the people.

There are many facilities spread throughout the nation. The primary facilities can be found in Philadelphia, Pennsylvania, New York and other cities. They are all accountable for keeping the economy steady.

The United States Mint serves various purposes. His initial responsibilities include providing paper and coin money to various businesses and the general public. However, it is also responsible for the security features of the re-issued currency.

The United States Government Mint is also responsible for bringing in recalled currency. Typically, funds are recalled when the government discovers an unclear situation.

Another factor is the quantity of gold and silver coins in circulation. The United States government mint must ensure a firm grasp on it.

The American eagle series of coins is the only type of currency that is available in both gold and silver. They are only available through approved coin dealers authorized by the United States Mint.

This facility is heavily protected and restricted to authorized personnel only. Because the government occasionally relies on its gold and silver reserves, this facility (valued at $100 billion) must be protected. The US government mint is the authorized issuer of all American currency.

Everyone is familiar with Fort Knox! It is one of the various facilities managed by the United States Mint. Fort Knox is, as you surely know, one of the most protected locations on the planet. Consequently, one may claim that the United States Mint is also the custodian of the nation's riches.

You can determine the value of a coin based on the condition of the mint mark and other variables. Another significant use of mint marks is identifying the mint from which the currency originates. Occasionally, this can also be a factor in assessing the value of a coin.

The minting method

1. Preparation of the metal strip with the correct thickness: zinc strip is used for pennies, whereas alloy strip is used for dollars, half dollars, dimes and nickels. Copper is coated on both sides of a thin copper strip to create a copper sandwich-like half dime.

2. Preparing round blanks: The strips are cut into discs nearly the same diameter as the final coins.

3. The spherical blanks are softened and cleaned by exposing them to higher temperatures in an annealing furnace, placing them in tumbling barrels and lastly placing them in rotating cylinders holding chemicals.

4. After washing and drying the blanks, they are sent into an upsetting machine to create elevated rims.

5. Inserting the blanks into a holding collar and striking them under high-pressure results in the production of coins. Approximately 40 tons of force is applied to press pennies. For larger coins, greater pressure is needed. The upper and lower dies are simultaneously applied to both sides of the blanks.

Mintages

A mintage is the number of coins of a particular denomination minted in a given year. This term frequently refers to all coins, regardless of their metal composition and some are referred to as collector coins.

The platinum Eagle coins are among the platinum bullion coins. Typically, platinum, silver and gold mintage coins have their ordinary versions coins in all values, proof versions of coins in all denominations and collectible uncirculated versions of coins in all denominations.

The figures marked with an asterisk are derived from recent sales statistics. Some of the information is based on unaudited US mint sales data, which differs from the final figures given by the US mint.

The collector coins are offered in four-coin sets, with unique mintage statistics reflecting the number of pieces sold in each set. Example: The proof platinum eagle number for the 2007 half ounce includes sales numbers for the 10th-anniversary platinum eagle set, which is listed separately.

Regarding the 2009 proof platinum eagle, it went on sale on December 3, 2009, with each coin containing 1 troy ounce .9995-purity platinum and being struck in proof condition.

It has a design of the symbolic idea "To Form a More Perfect Union," with the reverse portraying four diverse faces with hair and clothing woven together.

The coins that mark the beginning of a new six-year series of designs for the collectible platinum eagle depict the fundamental principles of American democracy as outlined in the preamble to the U.S. Constitution.

In 2009, the United States Mint ceased accepting orders for the 2009 American Platinum Eagle Proof Coin due to a maximum mintage of 8,000 coins.

Here is a list of some of the platinum coins minted:

- 1998 Platinum Canada Maple Leaf 1 ounce Coin
- 2007 W Platinum $50 Three Coin Eagle Set PCGS Proof MS-69

Regarding platinum coins, trading, buying and selling coins is the most recent financial trend. Be aware that selling a platinum mintage can be complicated and risky, particularly if you have no experience or understanding.

When you want to purchase a platinum bullion mintage, you must be aware of its value, age, rarity, and quality. However, if you have a broad understanding of the subject, there is no problem.

You can also compare prices online. Nothing is wrong with comparing the prices of platinum bullion mintages but you must be aware of the current market price.

Coins

People in the past did not utilize any currency to purchase necessities. They exchange their possessions at the marketplace for items they desire or need. As time passed, individuals learned the value of a currency.

They began to utilize money as a means to acquire goods and services. Because gold has always been regarded as a desirable commodity, their initial currency consisted of gold coins.

Silver And Gold Coins

Gold coins initially appeared about 643-630 B.C. King Croesus of Lydia introduced them. Electrum, a pale yellow combination of silver and gold that occurs naturally in Lydia, was utilized at the time. Then, people cannot differentiate gold from silver. Thus, the first gold coin was a blend of silver and gold.

HAVE YOU MET MONEY?

Around 560 B.C., they began understanding how to separate gold from silver. During this time, the first genuine gold coins appeared. While producing gold coins, they also began producing silver coins. Gold coins are highly valuable than silver coins. Therefore, the wealthy in the kingdom used gold coinage, while the working class used silver coins.

In 546 B.C., when the Persian army conquered King Croesus, they passed through the kingdom of Lydia. There, they discovered the gold coins.

They were intrigued by the Lydians' ability to produce gold coins and decided to master the trade. As they likewise viewed gold as a precious metal, they accepted gold coinage quickly.

As ancient Persia was regarded as one of the most progressive nations, the use of the golden coin swiftly spread to the rest of the world. Throughout the succeeding years, gold coins played an essential role in commerce. People from all across the world used gold to acquire goods and services.

In 1933, the use of gold coinage was discontinued. The cost of using gold coins as their currency has become prohibitive for nations around the globe. Currently, some nations utilize gold-colored coins that do not have gold.

The Silver Coins

For more than 160 years, the U.S. Mint was permitted to strike many denominations on silver coins. There are the dollar, half-dollar, quarter and dime silver coins in different denominations.

In 1965, however, a worldwide silver scarcity led to the production of a silver coin contrary to the president's directive. The silver content of dimes and quarters decreased from 90 percent to zero percent, while the silver content of the half dollar decreased to forty percent.

The final silver half dollar coin produced was the Kennedy a half dollar. No new half-dollar silver coins are being struck at this time.

Most collectors of pre-1964 Kennedy half dollars are keeping them. Also, because there were so many half dollars in circulation, most collectors now regard them as "junk" coins because they carry a negligible premium above face value.

The dollar silver coin was introduced in 1794 and removed from circulation in 1935. It was restarted in 1971 with the non-silver Eisenhower dollar, which was replaced by the Susan B. Anthony dollar coin in 1979. This was then replaced with the Sacagawea dollar coated in gold.

Values Of Gold And Silver Coins

Like other currencies, the value of gold and silver coins depends on different factors, including the amount of gold and silver coins produced, their age, rarity and condition.

The Age of Coin

First, a coin's worth is decided by its age. The older the coin, the greater it's worth. When evaluating coin values based on age, testing will be conducted to confirm the coins' authenticity and exact age.

Quantity Created

The quantity of gold and silver coins minted is another aspect that affects their value. The value of gold and silver coins with millions of copies is frequently lower than ones with a few hundred copies.

The state of the coin

The condition may also affect the value of gold and silver coins. Collectors will be far more interested in coins that are in pristine condition than coins that are damaged. The condition of the coins can have a substantial effect on their value. Collectors find it far more difficult to sell a worn gold or silver coin than a piece in good condition.

Uniqueness Of The Coin

Rareness is the most essential factor in determining the value of gold and silver coins. Those coins of which there are only handfuls remaining will have the highest value.

Although many gold and silver coins may have been struck in the past, they have been withdrawn from circulation in certain instances. As time passes, the remaining few coins will become increasingly precious.

Error Coins

US mint error coins are sometimes overlooked aspect of coin collecting. In the past, the market for error coins was minuscule but today, it is more popular than ever and people are eager to participate in this thrilling hobby. There is a lot involved in such a hobby and one should conduct a decent amount of research to appreciate US mint error coins fully.

Determining what a US mint mistake coin is can be difficult. The simple answer is a coin wrongly struck or minted at the United States Mint.

There is much more to the term but this provides a decent starting place for the novice collector. What matters most is that this is a terrific place to escape the monotony of typical coin collecting and achieve new heights in terms of rarity.

Since the beginning of the mint, there have been US mint mistake coins but there has been neither a market nor a desire to collect them. Early on, mistake coins had no value and were discarded or returned to the mint for replacement. However, many recognized the potential of mistake coins and seized these rarities in anticipation of what was inevitably to come.

For some, collecting mistake coins is about acquiring something others cannot. In contrast to regular coin collecting, there is a good probability that you own a one-of-a-kind coin if you collect mistake coins.

As there are believed to be many instances of practically every coin in the world, this is exceedingly difficult to achieve in the traditional form of coin collecting.

Overall, you should be aware that collecting US mint error coins is one of the fastest-growing hobbies on the market today. With the advent of new designs, mint errors are likely to be of exceptional quality and you should not miss them. Error coins are among the rarest and most precious coins in the world, frequently exceeding the value and rarity of regular coins by multiples.

Error coin pricing, like many other things, is highly dependent on the error coin's availability. Rarity has a significant part in determining price and value and the scarcity of many items in this pastime makes it an attractive investment opportunity.

There is also the issue of a coin's popularity about its value. Error coins that gain popularity will increase in value and price despite their true rarity.

A prime example is the 2005 Speared Bison nickel. The only design element on the reverse of this coin is a die crack that goes through the back of the bison.

Early in 2005, when this coin was discovered, its value soared and became an overnight sensation. This contradicts the notion of supply and demand, as there are more than enough of this coin for everyone who desires to acquire one.

Error coin prices will fluctuate within a few days, in part because of online auction sites. In the past, the market for mistake coins was tiny because there was minimal global marketing for collectors. This meant that collectors were at the discretion of local coin merchants and very few if any, mistake coins made it through.

Due to the Internet and online auction sites, collectors can access a potentially endless supply of mistake coins. This has driven the pricing of mistake coins to a point where many people are making a fortune.

Error coin pricing also depends heavily on the collector's willingness to pay. This is the most essential market factor. True, a trader can set any price he or she desires for a coin but if no one is ready to pay that amount, it serves no use. Dealers know that error coin prices are determined by collectors. Thus, they must exercise prudence when setting prices.

Proof Coins

The "proof coin" is a sought-after sort of coin in the hobby of coin collecting. They are specially minted coins with higher quality and specifications.

Due to their reflective features and composition, the qualities are significantly distinct from those of a conventional coin in circulation.

So why is a proof coin so distinctive?

The fact that a newly minted currency is not in circulation does not necessarily make it a proof coin. To truly comprehend the distinction, one must comprehend how coins are manufactured.

Proof coin structure differs from that of circulation coins. The coin is made when two dies strike and collide with the metal. The coin's design is engraved on the front and back faces of the two dies. In addition, the coin is struck twice, resulting in better detail than previous coins. By hitting twice, more metal is embedded into the die's template, creating finer lines and shapes.

In addition to its unique polish and die treatment, the proof coin has a distinct appearance compared to regular coins. The acid is put to the dies and the dies' backgrounds are polished. This gives the coin's background a mirrored appearance, while the rest of the design is frosted.

Proof coins provide a unique feature. The coins frequently have a letter, known as a mintmark, embedded near the year. The letter specifies the minting place of the coin. Examples of common locations include P for Philadelphia and D for Denver.

Proof coins in coin collecting are graded as "PR" or "PF." This is comparable to the evaluation of other uncirculated coins. The rating could range from PR60 to PR70, with PR70 representing perfection.

If the grade is below PR70, it becomes less perfect as it decreases. Occasionally, the grade may dip below PR60 if the coin was mistreated during production.

There is a proof coin variety known as "reverse proof." Reverse-proof coins closely resemble proof coins. However, the major distinction is that the field (the space) has a frosty-like quality, similar to tarnished metal. The raised pictures (raised gadgets) have a reflective look.

Because the name "reverse" is frequently connected with the reserve side of a coin, it is commonly believed that only one side of the coin has reverse proof qualities. However, both sides possess reserve-proof qualities.

In addition to proof coins, there are also prestige-proof coins. During the 1990s, these coins served as commemorative pieces, similar to the popular state quarter sets.

The coins are not inexpensive. Proof coins can cost anything from a few dollars to many thousand depending on the year or collection. Consult a professional coin collector or appraiser to determine the coin's worth.

Proof coins should be important additions to any collection of coins. Proof coins are crafted with greater precision, superior materials and finer tools. All they make collecting coins a trophy for any collector.

Numismatics

Numismatics is the collection of coins, precious metals and paper currency. Essentially, this entails investing primarily in older, uncommon coins. I am constantly contacted by numismatic salespeople who insist that this is the only way to invest in gold and silver.

Indeed, these coins are lovely. I enjoy owning, seeing and holding them and in strong coin bull markets, some of them perform rather well.

Observe that I said, "some" of them. Importantly, numismatic coins are only worth as much as someone is prepared to pay for them, based on their perceived rarity and excellent condition. That is all. A coin's actual gold or silver content typically accounts for only a small portion of its worth.

The pricing of numismatic coins incorporates three profit centers:

(1) the metal content or weight,

(2) the numismatic premium and (3) the dealer profit.

In contrast, silver and gold bullion and bullion coins only have one or two profit centers:

(1) the metal content or weight and

(2) the dealer profit (if you don't know how to buy at wholesale. more on this later).

Premiums for numismatics range from pennies to millions of dollars. Similar to how the stock market functions, the value of these coins is heavily influenced by the economy and buyer sentiment. Here is an illustration.

Today, a numismatic coin may be worth 10 times its value but next month it may only be worth X. In addition, dealer profits on numismatic coins can range from 18 percent to over 100 percent.

Before beginning to generate a profit, you must pay and overcome a substantial premium. If you are solely interested in owning a rare coin and not in generating a profit, that is OK but if profit is important to you, this is crucial.

If you're somewhat new to numismatic investing and you're working with dealers that have been in the industry their entire lives, what do you think is likely that you'll find great deals from them? My probability is close to none. Typically, under such circumstances, the one with the most expertise and experience prevails.

HAVE YOU MET MONEY?

There is no numismatic premium on gold and gold coins. A typical bullion dealer will charge anywhere from a few percent to forty percent or more above cost.

Coins are assessed by grading agencies to determine their market worth. The three principal grading services are ANACS, PCGS and NCG. Many experts believe that certain coin grading firms tend to overvalue or undervalue coins.

Some services are considerably more trustworthy than others. Again, it is a matter of perception of what defines "perfection" that virtually innumerable grading differences exist.

It is possible to send the identical coin to each of these three grading firms and receive a different grade from each. As previously said, it is all a matter of value perception.

No one likes to think about it but if, as some experts and economists are now predicting, the dollar crashes, unemployment skyrockets, many more banks fail. Things go from bad to worse.
and we are forced to use our silver or gold coins to buy, barter or trade with. which do you believe will be the most important:

(A) The fact that you possess a 1-ounce silver American Eagle valued at the current spot price of silver plus a small dealer premium; or

(B) the fact that you possess a 1 ounce Morgan silver dollar that is extremely rare and once carried a numismatic premium of $1,000 over the price of the metal itself?

Do you believe that the person you are trading it with will care so much about the coin's rarity in a situation such as this when you are in desperate need of cash?

Do you believe the numismatic value of the coin will remain the same in both good and bad economic times? That is your question to answer. I guess that it is not.

Here is an example that provokes thought.

Let's imagine you have 33 1-ounce American silver eagles (now worth roughly $30 each) in your right pocket and 1 1-ounce Morgan silver dollar (once worth $1,000) in your left pocket. (At current values, you would have paid around the same total for the silver in each pocket. approximately $1,000 apiece.)

Here is the query. In times of economic turmoil, which pocket do you believe would provide the greatest return? Which would get you further and provide greater long-term value? I shall defer to your response.

Unless you are a numismatic expert, I recommend collecting numismatic coins as a "hobby" rather than an investment.

Cull coin

A cull coin is any coin with defects or in poor condition. The phrase cull is commonly used to refer to all defective coins. It applies regardless of the precious metal composition, design or minting year of the coin. On the Sheldon scale, cull coins are often considered fair to bad.

Since there is no profile for a fake coin, I examine every raw coin I acquire. I've come across counterfeit old worn coins, new mint coins, inexpensive bullion coins and costly rare coins.

There aren't many counterfeit coins but detecting them is so simple that I verify every raw coin I acquire. I am always relieved when they depart. I detest discovering fakes and wish they did not exist.

HAVE YOU MET MONEY?

If I receive a coin in the mail, I verify its authenticity using the "ring" test. If the coin rings and appears correct, I rarely conduct more tests.

I perform the ring test in the coin shop before making a purchase. I've determined that if there's a problem with the goods, I'll bring it up in front of the dealer, despite the odd stares I generally receive from the counter clerk. I do not want them to believe I walked out of business, switched the coins and requested a replacement.

I strive to purchase coins only from vendors who guarantee the product's authenticity. Even yet, declaring that someone just sold you a counterfeit coin is a significant obligation. Before prosecuting someone for the coin, I must be satisfied that it is not what it was represented to be.

I have only returned to two merchants in my hundreds of coin purchases for selling counterfeits. I felt I needed a sturdy case with no doubt about the coin's genuineness.

When I discover a counterfeit coin, I am immediately faced with the dilemma of what to do next. As in every circumstance, there are many possibilities from which to choose.

1. Do nothing.
2. Call the authorities. Option 2 is comparable to option 1.
3. Contact the vendor. This can be similar to or more irritating than number one.
4. Report the counterfeit coin by calling the hotline.

I have discovered two categories of coin vendors. The first is anxious that they passed over a counterfeit currency without realizing it.

The opposing party seemed nonchalant about the occurrence as if they anticipated that a certain proportion of the fakes would be uncovered. Both, however issued refunds. I like dealing with the first variety.

When contacting a vendor about a supposedly counterfeit coin, I provide overwhelming evidence to support my argument. Most stores require that returned merchandise is in sellable condition. Unfortunately, if I cut the coin in two to examine the base metal, it will no longer be resalable, which I do not desire.

The authorities are mostly indifferent about counterfeiting because it is so tough to track down. Collectors must be their law enforcement. I must also admit that I have not yet located the number for the Counterfeit Hotline.

Ultimately, if you uncover a counterfeit coin, it will be your word against the vendors. It is difficult to demonstrate that you did not exchange their "genuine" coin for a counterfeit one to obtain a free coin from them.

Constitutional Silver

Consider for a moment what the world would be like if our monetary system were backed solely by gold and silver. This was the case not long ago but central banks and the capacity to debase our currency changed.

These central banks (e.g., the Federal Reserve and the Bank of England) have done nothing except pursuing inflationary policies, destroying our currency in the process.

 The government borrows from central banks; hence the interest on these loans must be covered by taxpayers. Let's examine the system of the Federal Reserve.

Instead of allowing these large banks to fail as a free market would dictate, the Federal Reserve has purchased the toxic assets on their balance sheets.

HAVE YOU MET MONEY?

This is inherently inflationary and serves no public purpose. The true market would say, "Tough luck if you fail," but they won't let the free market operate.

The Federal Reserve was established in 1913, following the first bank run that occurred in the early 20th century. It was founded under the pretense that a lender of last resort was required in the event of a bank run. It is false because it undermines a good monetary principle, namely, that banks should be able to lend out 90 percent of their deposits.

Since the establishment of the Federal Reserve in 1913, the value of the U.S. dollar has decreased by 95 percent. The Federal Reserve is the third central bank in the United States. The other two were prevalent during the 18th and 19th centuries.
The government printed so much of our first paper currency, the Continental, that the term "not worth a Continental" was coined to describe it.

The authors of the U.S. Constitution attempted to ensure that our government would never again be able to establish a central bank with the ability to create money out of thin air.

Our founding fathers were so astute that they ensured that only gold and silver coins could be used as currency by including this provision in the Constitution.

They were aware of the dangers posed by a government with the ability to print as much money as it desired. Therefore, they did everything they could to prevent this from occurring.

The Federal Reserve is, contrary to popular belief, a private bank. Indeed, they loan money to the government and the citizens pay them back with interest. A more dangerous fact is that the Federal Reserve was established to generate profits for a select few elites.

This is a grave violation of the U.S. Constitution forbids using certain items as money. Gold and silver are actual, intrinsically valuable currencies. Paper is not riches because it can be manufactured on demand.

There is no uniqueness in the paper. Inflation refers to the power to create as much paper money as wanted. While air is used to inflate a balloon, a printing press is used to inflate the paper currency.

Inflation occurs when more paper currency circulates without an improvement in production. Simply put, inflation is a hidden tax. It is a hidden tax since most people are unaware that their money's purchasing power is eroding.

Gold and silver will always be valuable assets. They may increase or decrease nominally but their value remains constant. Ancient Romans could purchase a handcrafted Toga and a pair of shoes for one ounce of gold. One ounce of gold may still purchase the equivalent of a decent men's suit today.

Personal Financial Statement

There are times when your bills continue to accumulate, regardless of how carefully you manage your credit card usage. If you find yourself frantically shifting credit card balances or calculating the minimum payment amount for each credit account, you may have more debt than you can manage.

If this is the case, you must take extreme measures to manage your debt. One option is to employ a debt counselor who will guide you through the necessary steps to become debt-free. On your behalf, the debt counselor will negotiate with your creditors for a reduced monthly payment to consolidate all of your debts.

HAVE YOU MET MONEY?

But what if you don't wish to consult professionals just yet?

You can build a personal financial statement and communicate directly with creditors. Those who want to reclaim control of their finances might take this debt-reduction step without needing to hire financial gurus.

Essentially, a personal financial statement is a document that lists all of your monthly or annual income and costs, depending on how much you earn and how much you spend monthly.

When you compile this type of financial statement before talking with your creditors, you may provide them with a comprehensive image of your present financial situation.

A personal financial statement is also an excellent method to begin budgeting and tracking your expenses, get out of a significant debt problem and create an effective savings strategy for the future.

Now, what are the steps you must do when preparing a personal financial statement? Here is a list of the essential components that you should include as a guide:

Your earnings list (Salary, benefits, maintenance, contributions from family members, etc.)

Your listing of expenses (Mortgage or rent, secured loans, taxes, utility bills, food allowance, etc.)

Your additional living costs (Vehicle maintenance, travel costs, childcare costs, insurance policies, medications, etc.)

Once you have totaled your income and costs, which should be coupled with your other living expenses, determine how much you have left to pay your creditors. You will utilize this to make offers to creditors. Your financial statement will demonstrate that your offer is reasonable and all you can afford.

As you build your financial statement, you can identify areas where you might reduce your living expenses. You may also consider alternative methods of raising your income, such as accepting a lodger.

If you believe your self-made financial statement is not sufficiently detailed, search for downloadable free forms online.

The purpose of a personal financial statement is to provide you with an overview of your financial situation. After doing so, you will be able to gradually evaluate what you can do to dig yourself out of your current debt scenario.

Barter

Barter involves 2 parties. Each party desires to trade with the other but instead of exchanging cash for goods or services, they will exchange the goods or services they already own.

That is, a product or service that one party possesses is exchanged for another product or service that the other party possesses.

Barter has its roots in antiquity because, as we all know, money as a transaction method did not exist until centuries after the use of barter. Using money or coins as a transaction medium was much simpler than transferring goods or services.

If a business has anything that can be sold and exchanged for cash, it can also sell in exchange for goods. Therefore, barter is simply defined as the exchange of products and services without using currency.

HAVE YOU MET MONEY?

When we were young, most of us engaged in bartering, even if we were unaware of it. For instance, if you have ever exchanged your comics for a friend's baseball bat or rugby ball, you have engaged in the practice of barter.

If you helped your neighbor paint her fence in exchange for her baking you a chocolate cake or if your neighbor helped you fix your car in exchange for borrowing your lawnmower, then you have engaged in the art of bartering.

For many years, huge corporations have engaged in bartering. Your organization should investigate it because it has many benefits and can lead to higher sales and financial savings in certain circumstances. As previously established, we have all bartered in some way or another but the barter business has only recently come into its own.

Computers can now track barter transactions and inventory, which has contributed to the expansion of this trading method. The phrase "barter economy" has emerged as a unique alternative to "cash economy."
Now, we have what is called "barter swaps." These organizations are responsible for the creation of markets and the gathering of traders for bartering. Barter transactions have also contributed to this industry's explosive rise.

Today, the barter sector is a multi-billion dollar industry and has become a very successful strategy for promoting company growth and allowing trade without using cash.

Chapter Three:
How Does Money Work?

IRS

Internal Revenue Service (IRS) is the main bureau within the United States Treasury Department. The agency, headquartered in Washington, D.C., is responsible for assessing and collecting most individual and business taxes.

Internal revenue refers to government money from domestic sources, as opposed to income from international (external) sources, such as fees placed on foreign merchants who sell their goods in the United States.

The government uses tax money to fund space exploration, national defense, maintenance of national highways and other public facilities, law enforcement, and public services such as education and libraries.

Individuals must file their annual returns or a request for an extension by April 15, while businesses must file their taxes (or requests for an extension) by March 15. In 2003, it was expected that the IRS would receive almost 130 million individual income tax returns and about 6 million corporate income tax returns, totaling trillions of dollars in tax revenue.

The agency is responsible for enforcing tax laws, disseminating the forms and instructions citizens need to submit their tax returns and offering information and assistance to make it easier for people to comprehend and comply with tax legislation.

The Internal Revenue Service dates back to the American Civil War (1861-65). By adopting the Revenue Act of 1862, President Lincoln and Congress enacted a federal income tax to generate funds for war expenses.

In addition, the act established the Bureau of Internal Revenue and the office of the Internal Revenue Commissioner to manage tax collection.

After ten years, the income tax was eliminated. Congress sought to revive the income tax in 1894 but the Supreme Court deemed it unconstitutional the next year.

The Sixteenth Amendment to the Constitution, that authorized Congress to impose an income tax, was not ratified until 1913, making income taxes a permanent feature of American life. To stress its commitment to "serve" the American public, the bureau was renamed the Internal Revenue Service in 1953.

What do IRS notifications entail?

You have just received a letter in the mail from the IRS. What does it want? Do I owe them additional taxes? Do I have difficulties with the IRS? Do not panic. Your tax issues can be resolved. IRS notifications are manageable.

The IRS sends millions of notices per year. These could range from default notices to tax return adjustments. Every alert identifies a problem and provides information on how to resolve it.

The specific collection process or CP number is assigned to the top of page 1 and the left side of the notice's tear-off stub.

These are the most frequent CP (collecting procedure) numbers:

- CP12: Minimum overpayment of $1 (Math error)
- CP14: Balance due (Math error)
- CP49: Tax paid in excess is applied to other taxes owed.
- Notice of intent to levy, CP90 (Final notice, sent simultaneously with CP297)
- CP297: Final notification ý Notification of your right to an audience (CP90 & CP297 are simultaneously sent)
- CP91: Notice before the garnishment of Social Security benefits (Final notice, simultaneously sent with CP298)
- Notice of intent to charge Social Security benefits (CP298) (Final notice, sent simultaneously with CP91)
- CP161: No mathematical error due to balance
- CP501: Balance due reminder note
- CP504: Critical Notice - Overdue Payment
Notice of Proposed Adjustment for Overpayment or Underpayment
Notice of Default on Installation Contract

If the notice describes a modification that you agree with, you don't need to do anything further unless you have a balance due. Please settle any outstanding bills by following the enclosed payment instructions. If you take the necessary steps right away, you'll only end up owing more in taxes and won't have to worry about penalties or interest.

Contact the IRS as soon as possible if you disagree with the notification and explain your perspective. There needs to be a phone number on the notification. If you prefer to provide an explanation in writing, you may do so.

Explain your disagreement with the notification and why you think it should be rescinded in your letter. To complete the notification, rip off and tape together the appropriate section. Within 30 days, the IRS will provide a response.

In most cases, you can expect to receive a second notice in response to your inquiry or further information. Don't hesitate to follow the notice's instructions to the letter. It is crucial to keep records of any correspondence with the IRS.

Central Bank

Central banks are at the center of a nation's economy and play a crucial role in the global financial markets. Their significance is especially essential to Forex trading, as they frequently serve as a benchmark for funds and trader activity.

If you are unsure as to why interest rate announcements can roil the markets, this section will help you have a better understanding.

What exactly are central banks?

Central banks are the institutions responsible for producing and managing the nation's currency. Most large central banks are independent, meaning they are unaffected by the government.

The functions of central banks include lending money to other banks and governments, printing physical currency and guaranteeing monetary stability through monetary policies.

The monetary policy of every central bank

A monetary policy is a method by which banks attain their goals. Maintaining inflation at a specific level (typically 2%) is a frequent purpose but there are other objectives as well. Central banks utilize different methods to achieve their objectives, including interest rate management and open market operations.

Inflation rates

The rate at which the central bank loans money to other banks is the interest rate. The country's inflation and currency can be affected by altering the interest rate.

For instance, if prices rise too quickly, the bank will seek to curb inflation by raising interest rates. If the economy is sluggish and there is an insufficient expenditure, the bank can reduce the interest rate to promote inflation.

Controlling inflation with interest rates impacts currencies as well. Increased inflation diminishes the purchasing power of a currency and causes it to lose value relative to other currencies. Conversely, lesser inflation boosts the value of a currency.

When analyzing the effect of interest rates on currencies, however, timing is a crucial factor. Increasing or decreasing rates may indicate the economic health of a nation.

For instance, if the European Central Bank (ECB) decides to raise interest rates following a recession, speculators may interpret this as a sign of European economic recovery and bid up the Euro. The opposite is also possible. Before making a trading choice, it is vital to analyze the background of each monetary policy announcement.

Open market requirements

Central banks can also intervene by conducting market operations. To achieve certain objectives, they purchase or sell currencies, bonds and even equities to regulate the amount of money in circulation. Consider the Canadian economy, which significantly depends on US exports.

A high Canadian dollar could be detrimental to Canada's exports, as Americans would have to pay more for its goods. Therefore, the Bank of Canada can opt to sell substantial quantities of its currency to lower its value and restore satisfactory export levels.

How do investors benefit from central banks?

You cannot afford to battle central banks if you are not George Soros. Therefore, the best action is to trade in the same direction as them. The wonderful thing is that they will not attempt to conceal their objectives; rather the reverse.

They wish to reveal their plans to gain assistance from traders in moving the market. Remember that the Forex is the greatest market in the world and therefore affecting the value of a currency needs the application of extremely powerful forces. Here, traders can assist a bank in moving a currency to a specified level.

Now, this is more important for long-term trading methods. Still, even for those trading shorter periods, it can be beneficial to determine the market's direction and establish a long or short bias.

Therefore, it is prudent to closely monitor central bank conferences, press releases and interviews to ascertain their perspective and trade accordingly.

Which central banks should you closely follow?

You should monitor any financial institution with interest in the currency you're trading. Forex traders must closely monitor the

Federal Reserve, which regulates the U.S. dollar because its actions influence the entire market.

Federal Reserves

The Federal Reserve Bank is not a government agency. In reality, it is a private business and international bank established by Congress in 1913. According to some, the 16th amendment was ratified rather dishonestly and illegally. In addition, Congress granted it the exclusive power to "print money" for the U.S. Government during the Christmas break of 1913, when most legislators were on holiday.

Before the establishment of the Federal Reserve, Congress had the authority and obligation to print our nation's currency. Since the Federal Reserve was given the authority to operate the printing press, the American people have been charged interest on every dollar ever printed.

This interest is not transferred to the federal government to support government initiatives or reduce the national debt. It is distributed directly to the "banking cartel family" that owns the Federal Reserve.

In addition, the Federal Reserve is responsible for the dollar's decades-long decline in purchasing power, which was caused by the issuance of excessive money. Since 1971, the US dollar has been unsupported by gold; it is essentially created out of thin air.

When this surplus money is added to the U.S. money supply, it "dilutes" it, causing the total value of the currency to decrease, hence necessitating more money to purchase goods; this phenomenon is known as inflation.

Here is the true kicker: the total national debt of the United States consists of interest still owed to the Federal Reserve, which the American people are forced to pay.
What then is the Federal Reserve's function?

HAVE YOU MET MONEY?

In addition to producing money, the central bank's stated function is to control the amount of currency entering the economy. It is a delicate balance between too much cash causing inflation and insufficient currency causing a recession. The Fed offers the counterbalance to keep inflation and recession in control "when functioning properly."

The Federal Reserve is a private banks group with Federal authority that operates in secrecy. They are not subject to government scrutiny or control and have no accountability for their conduct.

They operate largely in secrecy to maintain a steady flow of money between the extremely wealthy, financial markets, banks and consumers. This is accomplished as they respond to national and international political pressures.

Meetings of the Federal Reserve are always held in private, where decisions are taken without outside input. These decisions will ultimately and immediately affect the economic well-being of every individual in the nation.

Also, the Fed includes additional procedures or tools that can be utilized when appropriate. One of the instruments that will garner a lot of attention is the interest rates for banks, specifically commercial banks.

Many individuals find it perplexing or even dishonest when the Federal Reserve changes its interest rates. However, these rates will impact commercial banks that pay the Fed's rate to borrow money, which may or may not directly impact the consumer.

America's greatest problem is the Federal Reserve itself. Almost a century ago, our lawmakers betrayed the United States by turning over significant powers to the corrupt international financial elite, who have since undermined the health of our whole economy. Profit and power are the primary motivations of these "international thieves."

The banking elite consist of transnational bankers from multiple nations, none of whom are American. Consequently, they have no allegiance to American interests or the American way of life. Their commercial interests are hampered by nationalism itself.

Strategies

Before deciding on any action, if you're anything like me, you want to investigate and evaluate many alternatives. This has been the case for my wife and me throughout our pursuit of money.

Again, if you're similar to me, you've likely discovered that there are so many various ways to build wealth. It could drive you to insanity!

So who is correct?

I would try to suggest that most of the available financial information, techniques, etc. are useful in their manner. Before developing my financial approach, we tried different methods before settling on what has consistently worked for us.

Consequently, I am not one to assert that one must adhere to a particular philosophy. I encourage you to compare many "gurus" to see which one works best for you. To achieve financial independence, you can choose from different experts and adapt your plan to your specific needs.

For instance, some recommend avoiding debt when accumulating wealth. Others argue that spending the money of others (debt) is essential to being wealthy. So who is correct? They both have solid arguments and should be embraced (at the appropriate time) on your path to prosperity.

HAVE YOU MET MONEY?

Examine Forbes list of the 400 wealthiest Americans. You will discover that many of them are as dissimilar as night and day.

Some individuals are quite aggressive. Some are excessively passive in their efforts to accumulate wealth. So who is correct? Both viewpoints are sufficient to make you wealthy!

As you learn more about the wealthy, you should not be surprised to discover that they are all unique. However, this shouldn't discourage you from applying what they do. Simply continue to seek out the best strategies for you and adhere to them on your path to wealth.

Your ability to save rather than spend money greatly influences your beliefs about money and finances.

I refer to negative money views as "mental viruses." If you have a mind infection, it's like adding new applications to your computer - no matter how good they are, of course, they won't improve its performance.

Therefore, if people are not in the desired financial position, mental viruses are existing and we must eliminate these viruses - in this example, our negative money ideas.

Therefore, when we engage in financial healing, we eliminate the viruses and this needs examining and altering people's attitudes and beliefs around money and themselves. Therefore, we are eliminating negative thoughts and replacing them with positive ones.

Practical strategies for saving money

Secondly, there is the issue of what to do with the money - how to conserve money instead of spending it all.

Occasionally, savings are subtle. As a result of my history in financial services, I am aware that individuals who have purchased life insurance policies in the past may be able to obtain cheaper coverage currently.

Life Assurance Premiums May Now Be Less Expensive

This occurs due to two considerations. The market is currently more competitive and there have been significant medical advancements. Therefore, if you have a particular medical problem, it may no longer be regarded as highly, resulting in lower coverage prices.

In the late 1980s, ASSISTS, for instance, did not have quite the impact that was anticipated. As a result, rates have decreased and there are now many opportunities to save money.

To provide a further illustration of life insurance, the coverage that was pertinent at the time - perhaps to safeguard a mortgage or when you had a young family - may no longer be relevant now that the children have grown up and moved on.

Therefore, your amount of life insurance may no longer be required and you can be able to lower your expenses significantly.

Therefore, there may be alternatives to obtain lesser coverage that fit your present needs and save you money each month. Always investigate this in conjunction with a financial expert you know and trust.

Financial Recovery Analysis

First, you must eliminate any restricting money and finance ideas that keep you from saving for the future. This will avoid the sabotage of new, beneficial personal financial techniques.

Second, you need sound counsel on your present spending to see whether it fulfills your current lifestyle requirements. In our two cases, we discussed life insurance premiums but you must also analyze your usual expenditure categories.

Not Everything Is About Money

After addressing many negative money assumptions, you can come to a realization. Changing our beliefs about ourselves is frequently necessary. Perhaps you believe you are not deserving of excellent relationships, good health and riches.

Systems

Do you think a global financial crisis is imminent? If so, how do you intend to keep your family and valuables from vanishing? If you do not have one, you must acquire one immediately! This essay will describe my money protection strategy.

I am an optimistic person by nature. Nevertheless, I am convinced that the United States and the rest of the globe are in grave danger. Here is why I feel so strongly about this.

Federal and state governments' irresponsible and out-of-control spending pushes the nation to bankruptcy! I do not support either major political party! Each side is guilty!

Economic stimulus packages that didn't work, corporate bailouts for greedy corporations, real unemployment of 20%, skyrocketing costs of gas, energy and food, involvement in multiple wars or conflicts around the world and the Federal Reserve's perpetual printing of paper money as a solution to our country's fiscal problems are leading headfirst into an economic crisis known as

HYPERINFLATION!

U.S. Fiat Money

The term fiat money refers to "any money that a government declares to be legal currency."

*state-issued currency that is neither legally convertible to anything else nor pegged to any objective benchmark of value. Historically, the US currency was once backed by gold.

Paper dollars were simply receipts redeemable for a predetermined quantity of gold. This gold was kept under extreme security at Fort Knox, Kentucky.

President Nixon signed a measure in 1971 that removed the United States from the gold standard. Since then, our dollars have become fiat currency, that is, paper with no intrinsic value.

Throughout human history, various civilizations have embraced a fiat system. Every single one of these fiat currency schemes has failed!

As a fiat currency, the United States dollar has enjoyed a prosperous run but that run is set to end. The dollar's worth will continue to drop. Our money will be worthless!

Hyperinflation

Hyperinflation would be defined as "the economic condition in which the price of goods and services increases at an EXTREMELY, EXTREMELY rapid rate, resulting in the collapse of the monetary exchange system."

Is Hyperinflation Inevitable?

A growing school of financial thought holds that hyperinflation is not only possible but inevitable.

HAVE YOU MET MONEY?

If the U.S. economy achieves hyperinflation, our fiat currency, i.e., paper money will become worthless or as Robert Kiyosaki puts it, "cash will be trash!" The US dollar value is plummeting and a full-scale currency crisis is imminent!

We are currently experiencing the earliest stages of hyperinflation. Consider what is occurring with the prices of gasoline, oil, energy, food and commodities such as coffee and sugar. This is directly attributable to our fiscal recklessness!

Individuals will revert to using precious metals, such as gold and silver, in their transactions. In effect, gold and silver will serve as our new currency!

Why Are Gold And Silver Prices Skyrocketing?

Everyone is now aware of what has occurred with the prices of gold and silver on the market! They have reached all-time highs!

This is occurring due to two factors first, because the price of gold and silver has an inverse relationship with the dollar's value, the price of precious metals increases when the dollar's worth decreases! Smart investors who predict the arrival of hyperinflation are purchasing as much gold and silver as possible. High demand and limited supply result in a price increase!

In addition, many analysts predict that the price cap has a considerable distance to travel!

Problem With Gold As A Foreign Exchange

If you brought a gold bar to the grocery shop, it would be difficult for the store to give you a change! Consequently, using ounces of gold, gold coins and bars creates a significant challenge from a practical standpoint.

The issue with using gold as a practical exchange currency is that it is difficult to obtain in large quantities and small values. Before today, that is.

New Global Currency

Europe has embraced a new monetary system today. They use something known as a gold currency card. These cards are standard-sized credit cards. In the center of each card is a gold nugget that has been hermetically sealed. Typically, the ingots on these cards are. 1 gram, 1.5 gram, 5 gram and 2-gram denominations.

The Swiss government has confirmed these cards to be 99.99% kine-bar quality, the purest kind of gold.

These cards enable the usage of gold as a new global currency exchange system viable and realistic! Physical gold, unlike fiat currency, will always have value.

Gold has been a generally recognized form of value for millennia and continues to the present day!

Imagine this then. You will be able to use a gold money card in stores such as Home Depot. When paying for your products at Home Depot, you provide one of your gold currency cards to the cashier. The cashier swipes the card via a system that assesses the 1 gram gold ingot's current market value.

Gold-Backed Investment Accounts

Europeans are exchanging their paper currency for these gold cards. Instead of placing their funds in a savings account where their Euros are depreciating, people are constructing gold savings accounts.

It is crucial to realize that the goal of purchasing gold currency cards is not for speculative investment motives. The objective is not to engage in a game of purchase low and sell high.

Yes, gold (and silver) are currently on a highly bullish run. People have predicted that the gold and silver bubble will bust for almost a year. Despite this, the run continues to set records.

However, the purpose of holding physical gold is to develop a valuable reserve for the impending currency crisis so that when our money becomes worthless, you will have something of value to exchange for goods and services!

My Financial Protection Strategy

I am beginning to convert my liquid assets into gold and silver. My immediate objective is to invest 25 percent of my assets in gold and silver. Experts anticipate that the prices of these precious metals will continue to rise soon! Silver has been performing even better than gold.

I will open a Gold Backed Savings Account with a German company that manufactures gold money cards.

Most of my gold cards will be stored in a Swiss Bank account, the safest and most secure location on the earth. I will store a sufficient number of gold cards at home in a secure location for making purchases when cash is no longer practicable.

Methodology

As a result of the deteriorating economy and the shortage of viable jobs, many individuals have resorted to different tactics to earn money. Finding the right money-making strategy is a challenging option that many people must make.

There are many ways to create income and many people have turned to the Internet. Online business may be one of the most prevalent techniques to earn money on the web.

Working from home with a computer has made this highly tempting to individuals. There are many ways to make money online, including blogging, e-commerce, site design and development, etc.

Starting any business-related project can be a demanding undertaking. It needs extensive planning and investigation. Your head may be brimming with ideas and thoughts for your business but tragically, many enterprises have failed due to a lack of organization and insufficient planning.

Consider using mind maps to simplify your tasks and prevent you from falling into a trap. This concept has existed for a long time and is a very effective business tool. By utilizing them, launching a firm will be far less stressful.

What are Mind Maps?

- It is a technique for generating and organizing thoughts.

- A device that allows you to record your thoughts and ideas.

- It assists in unlocking the mind and expanding creativity.

- It employs a graphical representation of your thoughts, concepts or other related ideas.

The major theme is then subdivided into branches, which may be subdivided into smaller groups having the same concept as the central theme. This can be used to solve problems, outline ideas, collaborate on concepts, express creativity and organize enormous quantities of data.

There are many advantages to utilizing them in business planning. It is possible to cover every aspect of your business plan using maps. It facilitates the presentation of your ideas and the ability to see everything in one location will tremendously assist you in organizing your business.

You can organize, revise and restructure your thoughts and ideas to ensure that every element of your business is addressed. It will assist you in creating a more full image of your original concept. The mind map will represent the corporate strategy.

In the past, mind maps were created on a blank sheet of paper but there are now many books and software solutions available. When starting, it is advisable to begin with some instruction on the concept of Mind Mapping.

Modalities

You can use the Money Modality if you feel you're not getting enough money.

Not receiving any income?

How much junk do you carry in your wallet or purse?

You know the drill: receipts you meant to file or log into your finance tracker, lottery tickets you've been holding onto, 15 credit cards and other plastic membership or insurance cards.

Sometimes our financial investments are a mess. Even if you don't carry cash with you, your credit cards reflect the cash you would have spent if you did! So why the disorder? Why so much clutter? Things are being stuck in your wallet but they are not bills!

Purify that energy. Slim down your wallet or bag.

Remove ALL unnecessary things.

Align your bills so that they all face the same direction. Place the highest denominations at the bottom of the stack and the lowest denominations in the middle. Fold them with care, as if you were handling a baby's blanket.

Now, take a $100.00, $50.00 or even a $20.00 bill and store it in a separate section of your wallet from the other bills. Never use these funds.

Whenever you see something you want, you should tell yourself, "I could buy that right now if I chose to, because I have a $100," but you should stop making the purchase.

You are manifesting the energy of ALWAYS being able to purchase everything you choose! When money begins to come to you, as I am certain it will, repeat this method and place five $100 bills in your wallet and the next time, pack your wallet with ten $100.
Reduce the size of your wallet or bag so the universe can fill it. Try this for at least 30 days to make it a permanent part of your life.

Make a concerted effort to wipe out your wallet or pocketbook every day. Reduce the size of your wallet while envisioning a two-inch stack of $100 bills so thick that they would not fit!

Buyback Price

There are two ways for a company with surplus cash flow to return funds to shareholders. The first is to pay dividends. The second option is to begin a stock repurchase program.

HAVE YOU MET MONEY?

It is a scheme in which a firm uses its capital to repurchase its shares on the open market. The objective is to lower the number of outstanding shares, hence increasing the value of the remaining shares.

A company that initiates a stock repurchase program can accelerate revenue growth and payout larger dividends. Let's use an illustration to demonstrate. Ready? If necessary, please write it down on a piece of paper.

Company A is trading at $20 per share with 100,000,000 outstanding shares. In recent years, it has earned $2 per share and distributed $1 per share in dividends. In mathematical terms, this equates to $ 200 Million in annual profit and $ 100 Million in dividends.

Now, suppose that firm A distributes its whole profit to its shareholders. After allocating $100,000,000 for dividend payments, management decides to use the remaining $100,000,000 to repurchase its stock.

Meanwhile, the corporation will increase its profit by 5% to $ 210 million the next year. What effect does the buyback have? The table below will illustrate.

Considering the outcome, it is evident that stock buybacks improve earnings per share growth. Actual earnings increased by five percent, from $200 million to $210 million. However, Earnings Per Share (EPS) expanded considerably quicker.

It increased from $2.00 to $2.21, showing a growth rate of 10.5%. In the meantime, dividend payments decreased due to the falling number of outstanding shares. The corporation still pays a dividend of $1 per share but it now costs them $5 million less.

Assuming that the stock price remains the same at $ 20 per share, the EPS rise will be significantly greater if implemented over a longer time frame.

There are many lessons to be learned from stock buybacks. One is that investors will not need to be concerned if the stock price remains unchanged. The corporation can continue repurchasing its shares, thereby reducing its share count and accelerating its Earnings Per Share growth.

The second lesson is that stock repurchases reduce the cost of dividend distribution. As the number of outstanding shares decreases, the corporation can afford to boost its dividend per share even if the total dividend payout remains unchanged.

The third lesson is that the greater the number of shares a business can repurchase, the lower the stock price. This is beneficial for stockholders!

If the corporation purchases more shares at a discount, the same dollar amount will impact EPS growth. Consequently, investors frequently appreciate firms that commence stock repurchases when their stock price is down.

What kind of corporations can afford to repurchase their stock while also initiating a dividend? These companies frequently need less capital to run their operations and should be profitable. In other words, they own surplus funds.

Purchasing firms with positive net cash is also beneficial. Management may elect to repurchase its shares if it cannot find a better use for its cash.

Rate of decay

Time decay, frequently known as theta, is the rate at which the value of an option diminishes before its expiration. Extrinsic value is the option's value over parity with the underlying equity.

Since an option is a depreciating asset with a finite lifespan, the option's extrinsic value will diminish every day until expiration. This "decay" is not a linear function, meaning it is not distributed equally across all the remaining days until expiration.

As the options expiration date approaches, the daily rate of decay accelerates and continues to accelerate until expiration. At expiry, all calls and puts, options in the expiration month, in-the-money and out-of-the-money, must be devoid of extrinsic value, as illustrated by the charts below.

As time passes, the extrinsic value of an option declines.

Again, it is essential to notice that this drop rate is not linear, meaning that it is not smooth and consistent throughout the option contract's duration.

Approximately 45 days before an option's expiration, the contract's decay curve begins to increase. In the final two weeks before expiration, its value diminishes significantly.

This is comparable to a boulder sliding downhill. As the vehicle continues to descend the hill, it gathers more steam until it reaches the bottom.

By selling the option and retaining the underlying stock, the seller of covered calls captures the option's extrinsic value by holding the short call until expiration.

As previously established, the decrease of an option's extrinsic value over its lifetime is known as time decay. Time decay helps the seller out in the covered call strategy because the option's intrinsic value decreases over time.

Long-term stockholders who employ the covered call technique are given a second chance to benefit from their holdings. Besides making money when the stock price goes up, this method also provides above-average earnings during periods of stagnation and cancels out losses when the stock price goes down.

Covered call strategy design and implementation have been dissected. Keep in mind there are two entry points into the market. Covered Calls involve selling calls against shares you already own, while Covered Calls involving buying shares and selling calls against them are more complex (Buy Write).

I.e., an Initial Illustration

You own 1,000 shares of Oracle at a $9.50 price.

The stock price has been rather stable at its current level for quite some time, and your impatience with the situation is understandable.

When you sell front-month at-the-money call options, you're essentially giving up and letting the option expire worthless (November, for example). The strike price of the in-the-money calls would be $10 if the stock price were $9.50.

If the options premium is $0.50 per contract and you sell them, then your breakeven price is $10.50. Keep in mind that in a buy-write, the breakeven point is the sum of the strike price and the option premium.
Let's take a look at how things turned out for all three possibilities.

Taxes

HAVE YOU MET MONEY?

Taxes have existed from the beginning of civilization, including taxes such as transit tax, tax relief, income tax and any other terms that may before or follow the word tax.

Indeed, there is truth to the statement that we pay taxes from the moment of our birth until the day we leave this planet. Taxes obligate us to face it head-on, no matter what.

That is the truth and nothing on earth could ever alter it, for without it, the civilized world as we know it would cease to exist and no one would dare wish for that to occur.

People frequently complain about the taxes they pay; some even argue that paying taxes is a needless responsibility that we should not honor. Perhaps they are simply weighed down by the tax load or need to recognize the significance of taxes.

People like them may benefit from tax relief and they may be able to obtain it if they are willing to learn everything they can about taxes, their significance and their role in making our lives better.

Why is the government taxing citizens?

Why are we obligated to pay taxes and what do they include that will make our lives better?

These are a few questions we ask ourselves when we see the monthly, quarterly and annual bills from our governing institution in our inbox. Are taxes crucial to our daily existence? The response is unquestionably affirmative.

Taxes or tax money are the lifeblood of this civilization we refer to as government; without the financial side of taxes, no government could continue.

Tax dollars pay for government programs and activities required to keep the government functioning. Even conscientiously paid taxes with tax relief can make a significant difference in the lives of the people who look to their government for security, stability and survival.

There is no civilization, government, city or municipality in the world that does not collect taxes in some fashion, whether directly or indirectly.

There are taxes on all the commodities we enjoy every day. Yes, we pay taxes every day of our life but most of us do not even take the time to understand the taxes we pay every time we buy something.

Whether or not we receive tax relief, the funds go to the government's coffers when we pay taxes. There, information will be stored for a time before being audited and submitted to our legislators, government officials, senators and budget officers.

From there, our elected officials in the government will decide where to allocate this tax money or finances, setting priorities and the amount required to maintain a certain government agency or welfare program.

Taxes pay for social welfare, social security, public hospitals and all government entities that serve the public. The average person pays taxes through the purchase of basic goods, income taxes, tax relief and all the other taxes that we heard or read about, pay for and sometimes even grumbled about.

Some individuals complain while others are content to remain mute on the subject of taxes. While there may be a large number of people who are obligated to pay taxes, there are still a few or perhaps a large number who would rather not pay if given the opportunity.

HAVE YOU MET MONEY?

For a fact, not everyone is fortunate when it comes to their financial situation. In these financially difficult times, most of us would undoubtedly prefer a tax break or exemption if available.

Who in their right mind would refuse tax exemption? Indeed, there are activities, events and enterprises for which the Internal Revenue Service would grant you tax reduction or, even better, tax exemption but only if you follow specific rules to the letter.

You must visit your local Internal Revenue Service office to learn more about filing for tax exemption or tax relief. The next best thing to tax exemption is tax relief, which the government provides to taxpayers who are deserving of such a benefit. To qualify for tax relief, it is not necessary to be an exceptional individual; you must merely meet certain conditions.

There are many forms of tax relief offered and utilized by the Internal Revenue Service and each is designed for a unique set of criteria and people.

One sort of tax relief may be available to one group of taxpayers while unavailable to another. In this manner, our taxes are balanced and distributed equitably to their proper taxpayers.

These are only a few of the taxes that are being imposed on taxpayers and every one of them has been thoroughly researched, created, legislated and implemented to be practical and beneficial to both the government and the taxpayer.

Indeed, there are times when we, the taxpayers, would like a tax break, even if only for a limited time or for a percentage of what we already provide.

There is a remedy and taxpayers need only learn how taxes, their collection and rules and regulations work to qualify for specific privileges that would significantly reduce their tax burden.

One method is determining how to achieve or obtain tax relief. It's rather simple; you simply need to seek assistance from the nearest internal revenue office.

Charting

Charts are a common method for making stock trading decisions but the charts you employ and how you design them must be tailored to your specific aims and objectives. The disadvantage of using charts is that they can make you feel overwhelmed.

Various types of charts are available:

- Online free charting software
- Statistical software
- Online broker sites featuring graphs
- Chart-based financial software
- Investing plans that involve graphs

Individual chart settings present a difficulty for charts. Most online sources, including brokerages, have default settings. Who benefits, however, from these default settings? The key to effectively employing charts, regardless of origin, is customizing them to match your objectives.

The true purpose of charts is to determine when to sell, hold or purchase a new ETF (stock or fund). Sounds straightforward but do these signals align with your growth objectives, trading frequency, portfolio monitoring frequency and risk tolerance?

Consider, for instance, a Moving Average chart. This chart frequently displays two lines: a fast (F) average, which represents the average price computed over a short period and a slow (S) average, which represents the average price calculated over a longer period. In addition, the real total return price line of the stock or fund is displayed.

HAVE YOU MET MONEY?

According to conventional analysis of a moving average chart, a sell signal is generated when the price line falls below both the fast and slow lines.

In contrast, when it breaks through both lines, it is a buy indication and while it is in the middle, it is either a "watch" indicator if you are considering purchasing the stock or a "hold" signal if you already own it.

But what are the settings for the fast and slow periods?

How frequently are you prepared to trade?

Here are some thoughts:

- Daily or weekly - F10, S30

- Weekly or Monthly - F20, S60

- Monthly or Occasionally - F50, S150

While daily/weekly trading may result in significantly more deals than monthly or infrequent trading, the chance for significant losses is reduced.

The Full Stochastic chart can also be utilized to generate buy-hold-sell indications. This chart typically demonstrates two lines: an average price line derived from two types of moving averages (K + D) and a trigger line (T). When the average price line crosses the trigger line, signal generation occurs.

The Full stochastic graphic is typically read as follows:

A buy signal is generated when the price line cuts up through the trigger line in the bottom 20% of the chart; a sell signal is generated when the price line cuts down through the trigger line in the top 20%.

When the price line is between the bottom twenty percent and the top twenty percent, it is in the "watch" area and you should observe it for a few days before taking action, if at all.

Once more: How frequently are you willing to trade?

Here are some thoughts:

- Weekly or monthly - K35,D15,T10

- Monthly or inoften - K150,D50,T40

The second essential question regarding charts is, "Which charts should I examine?" Some charting software includes more than a hundred different charts and if you speak with ten people who enjoy charts, you will seldom find ten individuals who look at the same chart.

The other factor to consider while examining charts is how much time you have. If you have a portfolio containing eight (8) ETFs or mutual funds and intend to review twenty (20) charts for each one in addition to potential new "buys," you will need a substantial amount of time. You could view over 300 charts, which, at 15 seconds each, would take you well over an hour and possibly make you dizzy.

Regardless of the investment software or chart source you employ, you should be able to choose how and which charts to see.

MY chart choices should be compatible with any program and for what it's worth, I studied the following:

Moving Average - F20,S60
Stochastic Indicator - K35,D15,T10

These do not always agree with one another, which is fantastic since it forces me to study closely rather than quickly, yet I can still make a judgment in under 30 seconds. just use the charts to confirm or reject the outcomes of my investing program's technical analysis.

Again, the key to effectively using charts is to configure them to match your specific goals and to utilize only those charts with which you are comfortable.

There is little point in examining dozens of various types of charts when only a handful will provide the buy-hold-sell information you need.

Economics

Economics is the social science concerned with producing, distributing and consuming goods and services. Economics studies the behavior and interactions of economic agents and the operation of economies.

Economics is the scientific study of how societies allocate scarce resources to fulfill competing interests. The discipline of macroeconomics examines economic activity at the aggregate level. In contrast, microeconomics emphasizes the behavior of individual economic units.

Money is the economic medium of exchange for commodities and services. It is split into many degrees according to liquidity. M1 consists of coins, banknotes and certain checking accounts that are easily exchangeable. M2 includes all checking and money market accounts in addition to M1 and is less liquid than M1.

As a subset of macroeconomics, monetary policy refers to the activities done by the Federal Reserve System to control interest rates, the money supply or both. The Federal Reserve serves as the United States' central bank.

The purpose of monetary policy is to maintain economic stability. The Federal Reserve uses open market operations and reserve requirements as two of its approaches.

Theoretically, using these ways to limit the money supply will reduce inflation. Alternatively, if it is desirable to boost interest rates, the money supply can be increased by selling bonds, which will decrease bond prices.

Fiscal policy employs budget expenditures and tax increases or decreases to control the economy. Government expenditure and mostly taxation-based revenue generation are used to achieve fiscal policy. Theoretically, the economy will expand if the expenditure is increased and taxes are reduced.

Inflation occurs when prices increase. The Consumer Price Index or CPI is an indication of inflation. It is computed by comparing the current prices of household items to a reference year from the past. The rate of inflation is determined by calculating the percentage rise in inflation.

A budget deficit occurs when government spending is larger than government revenue. The reverse of a budget deficit is a budget surplus, which occurs when the government receives more revenue than it spends.

During the fiscal year, both the budget deficit and budget surplus apply. The fiscal year begins on October 1 and is a calendar year. The federal government uses it for accounting and record keeping.

When all the government's deficits from current and prior years are combined, the outcome is known as the national debt. The United States' national debt in 2008 is expected to be 10 trillion dollars.

With an estimated 300 million people in the United States, each person is responsible for around $30,000.

Adam Smith, Karl Marx and John Maynard Keynes figure prominently in the history of economics. Adam Smith is often regarded as the earliest proponent of free markets. He felt that the concept of an invisible hand led to the prosperity of individuals and nations.

Economic growth

Over time, the rise or improvement in the inflation-adjusted market value of the commodities and services generated by an economy. Conventionally, statisticians calculate this growth as the rate of increase in gross domestic product or real GDP.

The GDP or gross domestic product is the most frequent metric used by government agencies to evaluate the progress of an economy.

It is a monetary measurement of all the commodities and services in an economy over a specific period, typically a quarter or a year. GDP = C + I + G + NX or GDP equals the total of consumption, investment, government spending and net exports.

Conceptually, it is that easy but its use as a tool to measure an economy and deliver objective conclusions renders it an unreliable, highly flawed instrument that, for all practical purposes, should be dismissed each time it is presented.

For the sake of simplicity, let's assume that in year one, each variable had $100. The GDP is thus $400. This indicates that the total worth of all commodities and services in the economy for the given year was $400.

In the second year, consumption has increased by $1, while all other factors have remained unchanged. The current GDP is $400. It is expanding!

This is essentially what we hear four times a year in the news and from government organizations. They strive to boast to the public about their remarkable economic growth.

Despite this and contrary to all evidence and the numbers used in the example, around two-thirds of the gross domestic product (GDP) is consumption (private activity) and the second greatest share is an investment (private activity).

In addition to the government's limitations in taxes, regulations and other restrictions, about 80 percent of the GDP is the result of private activity.

It is unrelated to the government in the first two variables. If these were eliminated, consumption and investment would be significantly higher but that is not the focus of this chapter.

Despite the reality that the government is not responsible for most of the growth-inducing activity, politicians use their press secretaries to boast to the public about their fantastic job in fostering economic expansion, which is essentially dishonest.

Creating growth by giving back some of the money already stolen to increase consumption is analogous to a bank robber stealing $50 from everyone's bank account, mailing each account holder $10 and saying, "I enlarged your bank account by $10." This is illogical but the government, media and public enable it to become common knowledge.

Economic collapse

HAVE YOU MET MONEY?

You should be knowledgeable about economic collapse survival in the event of a recession. Essentially, survival can take various forms.

First, if the collapse is limited to the economy, you will be able to survive for at least six to twelve months on the financial arrangements we have previously made.

Now above that, even without income, your portfolio preparations should be able to generate additional money through multiple other ways simultaneously.

In the second case scenario, if the economic collapse involves money, you will need to rely on the physical supplies you previously stockpiled. Your acquired specialized knowledge and acquired talents will also help you survive.

Although a collapse of the economy may seem unlikely at the moment, you must know what to do in case it occurs. Currently, the economy's mechanics are very poor and a downturn might occur quickly. This implies that you should be aware of the many necessary preparation measures for this occasion.

If there is no fiscal collapse, there will be nothing wrong with owning some bank money. In a financial crisis that causes you to lose your work, you will have little reason to worry if you have a supply of long-lasting canned meals on hand. Also, educating yourself on precious metals and, if appropriate, investing in them is prudent.

A second essential economic collapse survival tip is to have enough money saved to pay your bills for around six months. Aside from that, there is a significant potential that bank closures would delay or perhaps steal your funds for many months.

It would be ideal if you had enough food, cash, precious metals and other barterable items in your home so that you could survive for months. Ensure that the money and valuables are effectively concealed in secure spots throughout your home.

As previously said, if a currency crash occurs, your money will be of little use. For economic collapse survival to be conceivable, "money alternatives" such as gold and silver are an absolute necessity. If all else fails, toiletries and tobacco are also excellent exchange mediums.

Water and food are, of course, essentials in the event of a catastrophic collapse of the monetary system. A terrific suggestion is a month's worth of canned meals that may be stored for many years if the expiration dates are checked.

These can be consumed every couple of years and regularly replaced with new ones. You can also search online for grains that are rich in nitrogen that is for sale. These grains satisfy your caloric demands and can be safely stored for at least ten years. These combinations with dried beans give inexpensive, full nutrition.

Considering the likelihood that water stations will close, keeping water in food-grade plastic containers will greatly assist. Essentially, water may be held in containers designed to hold beverages or food. Hoover plastic is the most viable option.

Economic collapse survival is possible as long as you know the many measures you can take to endure the worst economic conditions.

Macroeconomics

Macroeconomics studies large economies at the national or regional level by evaluating the movements of significant economic indicators and their interrelations.

What are the most important economic indicators studied in macroeconomics?

Gross National/Gross Domestic Product or Gross Domestic Product. This is the monetary worth of the goods and services produced in a country over a specific period. The GNP is the sum of the GDP plus any income produced by residents living abroad. It is one of the most significant economic indicators because it measures the country's economic performance.

ypically, it is released every three months. To obtain a more accurate picture of an economy's health, macroeconomists examine GNP and GDP in conjunction with other indices. For instance, a high GNP growth rate may mask the economy's decline since inflation rates exceed GDP growth.

The Inflation Rate indicates the growth rate in the prices of services and goods over a specified period. This is a key parameter since it measures purchasing power.

The greater the inflation rate, the lower purchasing power a certain sum of money has. Nevertheless, inflation can also result in wage gains. If salary growth exceeds price increases, inflationary pressures will be offset.

Macroeconomists also study deflation, which is the continual reduction in the prices of goods and services. While this may be advantageous to the client, it damages the economy as a whole, as decreasing revenues will force factory closures and increase unemployment.

Employment and Unemployment Rates These measurements assess the percentage of a country's total labor force employed and the proportion actively seeking employment.

These numbers are crucial because unemployed workers have less purchasing power, which can have a negative influence on other industries, such as retail and contribute to further unemployment.

A nation's economic growth can also be negatively impacted by high unemployment, causing it to deteriorate.

Payments Balance This indicator is considered the balance sheet of the national economy since it measures a country's trade balance or how much it earns from exports vs. how much it pays for imports and other financial operations.

If export revenues surpass import expenses, the balance of payments is considered positive and economic stability is demonstrated.

Microeconomics

This is a sub-discipline of mainstream economics that examines the behavior of individuals and firms in making decisions regarding the distribution of limited resources and their interactions.

In today's modern economic structure, the study of microeconomics is essential for aspiring economics scholar. In most cases, microeconomics is based on the cumulative study of how individuals and corporations or a combination of the two make allocation decisions, generally in markets where goods and services are traded.

This allocation or the optimum of limited resources through distribution often adheres to two standard theories: the Consumer and the producer. Consumers typically choose to maximize their available market preference given a limited budget or time constraint.

This is evident in the global economy, where consumers are always fiscally driven and typically make selections based on price and the time required to make their choice.

Producers adhere to a distinct spectrum. Producers' activities and decisions are generally motivated by profit maximization, with minimal capital expenditure or loss.

These two interactions are mutually reinforcing, as the producer's profit is generated by the consumer's interest in the producer's goods.

The customer and producer can enter different markets with knowledge of both sides. Product Markets and Factor Markets are the two primary types of markets.

Product Marketplaces are the most often encountered markets where consumers purchase goods from businesses or corporations. Herein lies the relevance of the Consumer and Producer Theory.

In contrast, companies typically purchase services from individuals on a factor market. These services may not adhere to the meaning of "purchase" but rather guide the employer-employee relationship. The sellers in a Factor Market are individuals who supply labor to corporations and preserve their money in banks.

Another important part of microeconomics is economic measurement techniques. When evaluating the efficiency of an economic system, many variables must be considered. These variables are designated as stock and flow variables.

A stock variable has no temporal relationship. Inventory variables are typically measured by necessity. Inventory, price, wealth and availability are often measured by necessity or quantity. Stock variables

play a crucial part in an economy since they establish a somewhat adaptable system for the consumer while still delivering an ample supply of goods.

Capitalism

The most common definition of capitalism is an economic system in which individuals manage their private resources and make decisions based on their self-interest. The alternative name for this economic system is the Free Market.

Most entrepreneurs follow the path of a capitalist because they can find more success in capitalistic countries, where private ownership permits the production of different goods and services and the retention of business earnings.

Individuals are also able to make decisions regarding their well-being under capitalism. They rely mainly on private contributions and organizational prowess, with the government playing a little role in the process. Often, business owners base their decisions on the government's engagement in the economy.

What Does Capitalism Mean To A Capitalist?

As a member of the Socialist community and I'm sure the same is true for most Capitalists, I've been able to distinguish the polarized thinking of the two sides.

Capitalists, for instance, prefer that the reward for a certain task be distributed to them FIRST before it is distributed to their subordinates based on the amount of work they contributed. In contrast, Socialists prefer that the reward be distributed equitably regardless of the amount of work or contribution to a task. Below is a more illustrative illustration:

Capitalists:

* Capitalists have a preference for leadership organization and the development of solutions.

HAVE YOU MET MONEY?

* They are more concerned with FINDING or CREATING chances than receiving them.

* Upon discovering an opportunity, they share the work with others and continue looking for more. They recognize time's IMPORTANCE.

* They employ an organization-based system in which they are only obliged to lead the most senior members of the many departments, instead of the entire organization.
Socialists:

* Socialists are followers; they like to be instructed and steered on what to do instead of making their own choices.

They prefer to WAIT for possibilities to present themselves or be presented to them.

* They prefer the work and opportunities for themselves rather than sharing them with others (since they think, "Opportunities are scarce!" primarily since they do not work on FINDING or CREATING opportunities for themselves).

They tend to slack off, which is why they prioritize working for a Fixed Income. (particularly noticeable among Government employees)

I may have come across as impolite, disrespectful and possibly offensive to most of you who are reading this section and some of you may have already pushed the close button but for those who are still reading, please try to grasp the point I'm trying to make.

The good things in life cannot be obtained without effort. What, thus is capitalism to me? It is simply the concept that hard work should precede the expectation of an appropriate reward.

Supply and Demand law

This law shows how, all else being equal, the price of an item tends to rise when its supply declines (making it rarer) or when its demand rises (making the good more sought after).

In contrast, it illustrates how the price of a product will fall when it becomes more widely available (less scarce) or less popular among consumers. This fundamental principle is central to contemporary economics.

"Demand refers to the quantity (quantity) of a product or service sought by purchasers, whereas supply is the quantity the market can deliver."

The relationship between supply and demand is rather straightforward but an essential concept for all businesspeople to comprehend.

Without understanding the link between supply and demand, one cannot perform effectively in the corporate world. If demand for a product is high, consumers will be prepared to pay a higher price for it and as a result, more suppliers will be willing to produce it because they can sell it for a higher price.

If demand is insufficient, the opposite will occur. A product's demand depends on whether it is a substandard or standard item.

As a country's median income rises, the sales of inferior items will decrease as more people can purchase the superior choice, while the sales of normal goods would increase.

Cultural shifts can also alter demand, such as the popularity of very baggy pants. During the early to mid-1990s, baggy jeans became extremely fashionable among younger adults, following the parachute pants craze. As the 1990s came to a close, baggy pants fell out of fashion and were replaced by tighter pants.

This resulted in a significant fall in sales of very baggy jeans and almost total depletion of sales of parachute pants. The supply can also be affected by external factors, such as a restricted amount of a product such as oil.

The cost of oil and consequently the price of gasoline has increased during the previous few years. China's substantial increase in oil consumption is a significant factor contributing to the rise in oil prices. Formerly exported to the United States, oil is now sent to China.

"When Venezuelan President Hugo Chavez threatened to stop oil supplies to the United States on February 10, it was widely acknowledged that this was an empty threat. However, this did not prevent the oil price from climbing for three consecutive days.

Most analysts believe that oil prices will not decline in the United States until there is a significant increase in supply, a dramatic religious conversion to conservationism or a recession " (Herbst, 2008).

Oil is a fascinating product from a supply and demand perspective because of the large number of factors that contribute to its price changes and it is also fascinating due to its restricted quantity on the planet.

Humans are stewards of the world but utilizing oil as a primary energy source often results in air pollution. To lessen the global pollution, we must seek out and accept alternative kinds of energy.

Gold silver ratio

Gold-silver ratio expresses the relationship between the prices of gold and silver. The ratio indicates how many ounces of silver are required to equal the value of a single ounce of gold.

The gold/silver ratio indicates how many ounces of silver are required to purchase one ounce of gold at a given moment. Examining gold and silver values dating back 4,000 years reveals:

• The ratio in the past has been 16:1 (it has taken 16 ounces of silver to buy 1 ounce of gold)
• Since the turn of the century, the ratio has been 30:1.
• In the preceding twelve years, the ratio has remained closer to 60:1
• In only the previous five years, the ratio has ranged between the low 40s and nearly 100.
• As of 1 March 2011, the gold-to-silver ratio was just around 40:1.

How can we capitalize on this fluctuation?

First, our buy timing is determined by the ratio. When the ratio is relatively large, we make fresh purchases with silver. We like gold when the ratio is rather low.

Finally, we take action when the ratio reaches extremes. When the ratio is high, gold and silver are exchanged. Then, when the ratio decreases, we exchange silver for gold. We exchange silver for gold when silver has appreciated more rapidly than gold.

The gold is then exchanged for silver when silver becomes "cheap" relative to gold. Each time this cycle - gold to silver and back to gold - is repeated, our ounces rise. This is the entire objective. For instance:

Suppose you owned one ounce of gold and the ratio of gold to silver increased to 80:1. One ounce of gold would be exchanged for eighty ounces of silver. When the ratio fell to 40:1, you would exchange your 80 ounces of silver for 2 ounces of gold, doubling the number of ounces in your possession.

Next, we purchase the form of silver or gold that gives the greatest potential for profit. During times of high demand, investors often bid 20 to 40 percent or more above the item's intrinsic value.

Then, we can exchange the things with high premiums for those with lower premiums, capturing most of the difference and transforming it into additional ounces of metal.

Moreover, there are no additional costs associated with employing this method. Utilizing this ratio technique is preferable to the alternative, which is to wait for the price to grow.

Mint ratio

The mint ratio, commonly known as the gold/silver ratio, is calculated by dividing the price of an ounce of gold by the price of an ounce of silver.

This ratio shows the precious metals' exchange rate. It is sometimes used as a proxy for market risk and to determine if risky assets are over- or undervalued.

A present for someone who has everything! This is something we have all heard before but could it be true? True, giving is superior to receiving but in this case, receiving is on par with or even superior.

1. According to experts, to increase your chances of successfully building wealth, you must invest in multiple areas, including 10 to 20 percent in precious metals. Since 2001, gold prices have increased by about 196%, exceeding the Dow by 400%.

Who wouldn't want to hold a commodity investors generally turn during a financial crisis? Gold has always been the haven for investors fleeing volatile markets.

2. In these unpredictable markets, experts now forecast that the price of gold will reach $2,000 per ounce or higher. This makes gold an exceptional investment for profit and security in economic and market volatility.

The value of stocks can decline and firms can fail, leaving you with worthless pieces of paper. Due to low-interest rates, cash may lose its capacity to gain value. With bonds, your funds are invested for the duration of the period.

When property values decline, it is possible to lose years of equity. Other than gambling, how many other ways are there to lose money?

Okay, so that's the information on gold but how does silver compare?

3. Many features and capabilities of silver are particularly beneficial to the industrial industry. Silver is utilized in many industries, including electrical appliances, medicinal products, microcircuits, superconductors and 90% solar cells.

Solar panel demand will explode with the anticipated increase in demand for newer, more efficient renewable energy sources. The amount of mined silver that is available above ground decreases annually.

4. The correlation between silver and gold prices is approximately 1:70. However, this ratio might fluctuate. Traders, investors and purchasers often examine the gold-to-silver ratio. As the price of gold rises, silver will inevitably follow and so should you.

So, what should I do next? The prudent action would be to purchase gold and silver but what should one purchase?

5. You are not required to buy bullion bars. There is a superior choice. Purchasing collectible gold and silver coins in flawless condition is the best way to begin.

Depending on your budget and how much you like the recipient, you can give anything from a single silver coin to a collection of gold coins.

These coins are priced according to their numismatic and collectible value.

6. Coins have both a face value and a value per ounce. As a result, they are insulated from falling commodity prices and will be exchanged as collectible coins of exceptional quality.

You also have the rising value of the coin's basic metal content. Gold and silver bars can only rise or fall with the value of the base metal.

It is simple to keep and present seven coins. You can easily add this year's new releases as your collection grows, making gift-giving simpler.

You might begin with the children's gift sets, which will cover all of your young nieces and nephews. A dated, collectible silver coin in flawless condition would make the ultimate christening gift.

There are different options to sell your coins or bullion, including selling the bullion to a reputable trader who will provide you a lower price than they would if you were to purchase it from them.

One of the most popular methods is to sell on an online auction site. People tend to get carried away when bidding on rare collector coins in mint condition and the same is true when selling your bullion.

Assets

Webster's Dictionary defines an asset as a sufficient property to cover debts and bequests. This tells you nothing about what you can be sued for or what a creditor can use against you in court.

If you owe the IRS, child support, court-ordered fines or federal student loans, they can essentially place a lien on any asset you own.

This includes residences, salaries (disability, genuine employment and unemployment), automobiles, boats, trailer or mobile homes, bank accounts, and whatever else they may obtain. This does not indicate that they will attach these assets to your debts. It only indicates that they can.

Now, let's address the remaining creditors. To whom you owe the money will determine the collateral they attach to your obligation. This depends greatly on whether you work with a debt-buying agency or a contingency-based firm.

If the judge permits it, they can attach any assets they deem appropriate if they purchased the debt. On a contingency-based agency, they can only seize assets that the original creditor authorizes. (If you haven't read the section on determining which agency you are working with, please do so now and return.)

The wealthy acquire assets, while the poor and middle-class purchase goods. We have all heard this before but how can we recognize a valuable asset?

Understanding the definition of an asset is the first step. I like how Rich Dad defines an asset. A liability takes money out of your pocket but an asset puts money into your pocket.

Many individuals view their property as an asset. This is accurate, although it is unclear whose asset it is. If you have a mortgage on your home, it is likely an asset of your bank and not yours.

Real estate, business and paper assets are the three asset classes. Your biggest asset is you. You may be your greatest liability. How an acquired business is managed determines whether it becomes an asset. Your work ethic, dedication and expertise contribute to the firm's success.

To be a good investor, you must first focus on yourself. Also, it is essential to evaluate your strengths and weaknesses and purchase assets accordingly. For instance, if you dislike painting, doing repairs or doing yard maintenance, purchasing a fixer-upper rental home may not be your best investment.

Liabilities

Liability generally refers to the acceptance of legal or financial responsibility for anything. You are responsible for a debt or demand for which you are considered liable.

Individuals or organizations may be held accountable for various debts and legal responsibilities. Therefore, it is generally prudent to comprehend your liabilities and how they may affect you. Thus, you may safeguard yourself, your finances and your possessions.

Legal Responsibility in Suits and Claims

In lawsuits and claims, responsibility is the possibility of being held legally liable for someone else's loss. Joe's injuries would be your responsibility if he entered your land and fell through a hole you neglected to cover.

Joe might sue you for any medical expenses incurred due to his injury. Joe may also utilize your services if he is wounded and cannot work.

There are many methods to incur a responsibility. You may incur responsibilities if you sell any product or service. Let's assume that Shane hired Sally to balance his books but she performed a poor job. Not all of Shane's bills were paid, resulting in financial losses. Shane might sue Sally because she made herself liable for some of his debts by agreeing to perform a job for him.

This is why there is something known as liability insurance, which protects against obligations incurred due to specific actions. A homeowner's policy will protect you against liabilities unique to property ownership, such as Joe's lawsuit.

A business insurance coverage will cover company-related losses. Sally may have insurance that would cover the cost of a lawyer to defend her against Shane's lawsuit.

Business and Everyday Life Liability

The notion of guilt is vital to our legal system. Under our legal system, individuals are considered to assume responsibility or blame for their conduct.

For instance, it is anticipated that you will drive your vehicle carefully; if you drive carelessly and cause an accident, another motorist and his insurance company could sue you.

Therefore, an important objective is to promote personal accountability. Our legal system also includes mechanisms designed to shield individuals from certain liabilities.

The purpose of a company, including a limited liability corporation, is to protect investors and management from liability. By establishing one, an entrepreneur can shield his home and personal bank accounts from lawsuits originating from commercial operations.

Commodity

A commodity is a "good" for which demand exists. There are "soft commodities," which are grown things and "hard commodities," obtained by mining or extraction. There are also those without an underlying product.

To further illustrate the distinction, we have commodities in Agriculture, Energy, Equity Index and Forex or FX as it is more commonly called. Metals and interest rates are only two examples. Different exchanges trade different commodities.

To further dissect these commodities, I shall begin with agriculture. Initially, "Grains and Oil seeds. Corn, wheat, soybeans, soybean meal, soybean oil, crude palm oil, oats and rough rice are all available.

In the same section as "Agriculture" is "Livestock." This comprises live livestock, feeder livestock, lean hogs and frozen pork bellies. People laugh at pork bellies but what do you think happened when commodity trading societies heard the term "Swine Flu" for the first time? Consider this carefully.

There exists "Dairy." There are many "Milk," including Milk powder, whey and butter. Cocoa, coffee, cotton and sugar are "softs." "Forest": Timber and paper products. No more "Agriculture"; let's proceed.

The following heading I move to is "Energy." Due to its prominence in the news and its impact on our wallets, I'm confident that most people find this topic intriguing. The first entry in the energy section is "Crude Oil.

"But did you know that there are six other oils listed under the term Crude Oil in addition to "Light Sweet Crude Oil"? Which, by the way, closed at 90.85 per barrel on the floor on Friday but is at 91.10 on Globex. More about Globex will follow MUCH later.

Also, there is "Gulf Coast Sour Crude" for one. I have never deliberately consumed oil. So how do you determine whether food has gone bad? Considerable food for thinking.

A second heading is FX or Forex. This is an independent universe. Under this section, the primary titles are "G10 Currency Pairs" and "Emerging Market Currency Pairs." The G10 consists of the top 11 industrialized nations. However, the name has never been changed.

Currency pairs are the comparison of one of the top 10 currency dollars against another dollar, often the U.S. Dollar or USD, as it is commonly referred to and traded. Emerging Market Pairs is what it implies.
Whether or not immigrants are achieving success, forex trading is a massive market that requires careful consideration if one wishes to participate. Not that any other Commodity is less deserving but the fact that different countries' currency rates are followed is scrutinized closely.

The following heading is "Metals." What comes to mind initially? GOLD. Gold is referred to as "Precious." Similarly titled are silver, platinum and palladium. Copper is listed as "Base" in the encyclopedia. The second is Uranium.

Uranium cannot be taken into actual possession. Uranium futures are a hedging instrument for uranium producers and consumers..

Investment Vehicle

A product employed by investors in the expectation of generating profits. Low-risk investment vehicles include certificates of deposit

(CDs) and bonds, whereas high-risk investment vehicles include stocks, options and futures.

It makes sense to invest your money if you know where you will be investing. There are different investment options available. Your investment should also be dependent on your risk tolerance, investing style and financial goals but you should first familiarize yourself with the various investment vehicles accessible.

Investing is comparable to purchasing a new vehicle because there are many models and payment methods. If you were to purchase something new, you would not purchase something you had not previously researched or tested. Typically, you solicit opinions, research, and evaluate various models before making a final selection.

The previous chapter reviewed the factors to consider when developing an investment strategy. This section will delve a bit deeper into how you can apply these building pieces to an unlimited number of investment opportunities.

Because we wish to keep things simple, we will avoid all exotic assets and concentrate on the three most common: stocks, bonds and cash.

Stocks

When you own shares of a company, you own a portion of that company. It may consist of only a few shares and thus a very small portion, yet it is still a portion of ownership.

Technically, you own a portion of the company but it doesn't mean you can go to the headquarters and tell the CEO what to do or carry out a computer; it merely means you have a share in the company's present and future earnings.

Generally speaking, if the corporation has a positive net income, the shareholders may get a dividend, which is a fraction of the company's net income per share. There are various sorts of stock but the type in which we have the greatest interest is common stock.

In addition to having the possibility to earn dividends, common shareholders have the right to vote on certain company matters. You may also hear stocks referred to as "equities," as stock ownership indicates equity in the corporation.

There are many methods for determining whether a stock is overvalued or undervalued but they are outside the scope of this study.

Many common stock types (e.g., small cap, mid cap, large cap, growth, income, etc.) are associated with varying degrees of risk. These classes will be discussed in further detail when we cover diversification and risk management.

Bonds

Bonds also referred to as "debt instruments," are the primary method through which businesses and all levels of government borrow money.

When you buy a bond, you are essentially lending money and when the bond matures, you should receive interest payments in addition to the principal (the amount you "loaned").

In reality, bonds are rarely purchased and held until maturity; rather, they are regularly bought and sold on the secondary market over the bond's life, which means that even the face value might fluctuate.

This is a gross oversimplification of how bonds operate. As with stocks, there are valuation methods to assess whether a particular bond is a good investment or not but it is sufficient for our purposes that you have a basic understanding of the distinction between stocks and bonds.

Cash

In personal finance, when someone mentions a certain amount of cash in their portfolio, they are solely referring to the fact that their portfolio contains "cash" type investments. With these investments, the principal (the amount invested) does not fluctuate in value.

People commonly regard money markets, certificates of deposit and regular savings accounts as cash investments (while technically the value of money market shares can drop, they are virtually always stable).

Investment Time Horizon

This can be described as the length of time an investor plans to hold an investment before withdrawing funds. Investment objectives and strategies substantially determine time horizons.
Having a time horizon is an essential need for investing.

We must have a solid understanding of our breakeven point for a specific venture. Without realizing it, we may make incorrect investments.

Time horizon refers to the point at which investment must stop to be used for something else. Therefore, it might refer to when we need money to pay for necessities such as rent and food, make a down payment on a significant purchase or invest in something else. Also, it often has many points, such as a loan's succession of payments.

When investing with a time horizon in mind, the objective is to match the expected payments with the actual returns. For instance, assume you must pay $10,000 for a ring you wish to purchase in six months.

This money could be invested in a bond with a maturity date of six months. Thus, the bond payment and jewelry payment have been matched.

If, on the other hand, you invest the funds in a 12-month bond, you will certainly not have the funds! It would continue to reside in the bond. This example may seem absurd but it demonstrates that we must be mindful of our time horizon.

Therefore, we begin investing by asking ourselves when we will need the money. Will it be in one year, five years, twenty years or much beyond in the future? Typically, it will be all the above.

Typically, we have various financial objectives, resulting in multiple periods. Consider each of these separately. Once you have determined your time horizon, you may search for the most suitable investments.

Financial Statement

Financial statements are regarded as the culmination of transactions between a particular firm and other businesses and individuals. In transactions, sales, purchases and general cash flows are included.

There are many forms of financial statements, including the balance sheet, income statement, cash flow statement and statement of changes in owner's equity. This essay will cover the balance sheet, one of the most significant financial statements.

Financial Statement

HAVE YOU MET MONEY?

The balance sheet is a statement that summarizes the financial condition of a business at a specific point in time, typically at the end of an accounting period. It illustrates the company's assets, liabilities and owners' equity.

The equation for the balance sheet is Assets = Liabilities + Owners' Equity.

Since the two sides of the equation are equal, the statement is called a balance sheet.

Assets are the economic benefits an organization will gain and manage due to past transactions. The tangible assets of a business are cash, accounts receivable, inventory and equipment. Assets can be divided into current and long-term categories.

Current assets, such as cash and accounts receivable, are assets that are or can be converted to cash or provide value to the organization within a year.

On the other hand, long-term assets, such as land, inventory and equipment, are paid off and will benefit the business over a lengthy period.

On balance sheets, accumulated depreciation is used to show how the cost of long-term assets is "consumed" during the operation of a corporation.

The expense is amortized over the asset's useful life. For instance, if a piece of machinery costs $50,000 and has a useful life of 20 years, the equipment's accumulated depreciation for the first year is $2,500.00.

Simply put, liabilities are the amounts owing to other organizations, such as the transfer of assets or the provision of services. Also, liabilities consist of both present and long-term obligations.

Current obligations include accounts payable, notes payable, current maturities of long-term debt and payroll taxes due within one year. Long-term debt is debt that is repaid over a prolonged time frame.

Owner's equity, also known as net assets, is the remaining ownership right after subtracting liabilities. Shares of common stock, additional paid-in capital and retained earnings are examples of owner's equity.

The company issues common shares as an investment opportunity. In corporations, for instance, stockholders are the ultimate owners, claiming all assets after liabilities and preferred stock claims have been paid.

Additional paid-in capital is the amount paid by the investor that exceeds the stated value of the sold shares. Lastly, retained profits represent the net income not dispersed as dividends to shareholders or an organization.

So, what is a balance sheet's function? First, business owners utilize balance sheets to evaluate the business's strength and potential.

For instance, is the business prepared for expansion? Or should the company take quick action to bolster its financial reserves? In addition, balance sheets illustrate trends, particularly in the accounts receivable and payable areas.

For example, is debt in payables being paid and is debt in receivables being received on time? Finally, banks, investors and vendors review balance sheets to assess the amount of credit they will extend to an entity.

Asset management

There are many definitions of "asset management," but most emphasize financial factors. Some are based on the evolution of maintenance management systems, others on the management of manufacturing floor equipment configurations and still others on monitoring network equipment or the whereabouts of rail cars and containers.

Asset management is "a systematic procedure for identifying, categorizing, monitoring, maintaining, operating, improving and replacing the organization's physical assets cost-effectively," regardless of the specific scenario or application.

To be genuinely effective, the asset management process must be based on generally accepted accounting standards and backed by strong business practices and financial savvy.

It can give management a powerful instrument that can be used to make better short- and long-term planning decisions. Therefore, every organization should consider adopting it.

I choose to define asset management more dynamically, embracing each of the four important components listed below:

A tool for generating and maintaining key management data for use internally by the organization and externally with its customers and suppliers (such as installed base or maintenance entitlement data).

A thorough method for acquiring, validating and integrating data into enterprise information systems.

A versatile system that permits either the manual or electronic data capture and reconciliation.

A tool that provides accurate and intelligent reporting of vital business and operational data.

Asset management is not limited to the identification and inventorying of IT and related equipment; it is the process of maximizing the productivity and profitability of the company's assets. In addition, it is not a system that can be purchased; rather, it is a business discipline enabled by people, processes, data and technology.

Market makers

A market maker is a member of FINRA (Financial Industry Regulatory Authority) originally known as the NASD (National Association of Securities Dealers) (National Association of Securities Dealers).

Market makers quote to purchase and sale prices for financial commodities, profiting from the difference between the bid and offer spread.

The market maker is compensated for providing market liquidity. A market maker is also connected with regulation 15c211, as a market maker must file a 15c211 to trade any given security.
When you purchase or sell a stock or place an order with your broker, the transaction is completed in a matter of seconds. The process is very straightforward for the buyer or seller but the action occurs behind the scenes, where market makers match the buyer and seller.

Without a market maker, it is extremely improbable that you will find a buyer or a seller for an exact quantity of shares at any particular moment.

Even when no other bidder is lined up, the market maker will purchase a large number of shares from a seller. By doing so, they assume substantial risk. If the stock's value declines while they have it, they will lose a substantial sum.

Market makers maintain a spread on every stock they purchase to avoid this. The difference between the asking price (the price they buy it for) and the bid price may be merely $0.05. (the price they offer to sell it for).

They sell to and purchase from their clients in foreign marketplaces, where most transactions are over-the-counter.

Offering additional liquidity decreases the cost of transactions for clients and increases the profitability of trades. They would have to accept a low price for the stock or cannot trade it at all if not for the market maker.

In the United States, the AMEX and NYSE each have a single exchange member, sometimes known as a "specialist" for certain security, who functions as the market maker.

The specialist ensures the needed level of market liquidity, prevents excessive volatility and takes the opposite side of trades when there are imbalances between buying and selling customer orders. Consequently, the specialist has access to trade execution benefits.

On the NASDAQ and other U.S. exchanges, many market makers are competing for given security. They are required to purchase and sell at prices corresponding to their published bids and offers and do not gain a specialist's benefits.

According to proponents of the formal market maker system, market makers contribute to the liquidity of the stock and commodity markets by undertaking risk and taking short or long positions in the hopes of making a profit.

Market makers on the London Stock Exchange can buy and sell stocks at all times. Each stock is always obligated to trade with at least two market makers.

Market manipulation

As an individual investor, you lack the financial resources to influence the market. However, there is no reason why you cannot profit from the market manipulations of other parties.

Market manipulation is unlawful, but you would be surprised at how many people seek to do so in markets with little activity.

A prime illustration is the silver market.

As a result of one of the largest short squeezes in history, I predict silver prices will experience a massive increase.

It will not occur today, tomorrow or in the next month. However, I anticipate it will occur within six to eight months.

The silver market is underdeveloped. The aboveground supply is around 600 million ounces and silver demand exceeds supply annually.

On the other hand, gold has an annual excess of over 4 million ounces, and every major nation possesses masses of gold that could be readily dumped back onto the market.

All these factors make silver an ideal commodity for price manipulation. If any large silver traders opted to sell silver short, the price of silver would fall precipitously.

HAVE YOU MET MONEY?

To maximize the damage, these large dealers would engage in short selling between 1:00 and 2:00 in the morning, when the market is most illiquid.

As soon as they sold their massive short positions and the price began to fall, stop-loss orders would be triggered. These bets would be liquidated, precipitating a further decline in silver. This second decline would impact an additional group of stop-loss positions and the price would continue to decline until most sell-stops were reached.

This occurred in May, when the price of silver reached $15 per ounce. A small number of large silver dealers shorted silver, causing the price to fall below $10 within a month. These traders greased the skids by continuing to sell silver short of exacerbating the downward trend.

According to the weekly Commitments of Dealers Report (COT) published by the New York Commodity Exchange (COMEX), the eight largest silver traders own 54.4% of the total net short positions.

Nearly 37% or 35,626 net short futures contracts are controlled by the four largest traders.

Considering that each contract represents 5,000 ounces of silver, these four traders control 178.13 million ounces of silver, which is more than the COMEX possesses in its vaults.

However, this purposeful attempt to reduce the price of silver may easily fail.

Imagine that North Korea started firing missiles at random. The political unpredictability would increase the price of silver, maybe to between $17 and $18 per ounce. Both the major short holders and COMEX would be in a precarious position.

As the price of silver increased, these dealers would need to respond to margin calls. This would need them to find the cash to infuse into their accounts as their positions begin to lose money. (They could be trading on leverage at 20% but in this case they could easily be down 50%.)

And when their available funds ran out, they would have to repurchase silver (at a loss) to continue meeting their margin calls.

The price would increase if they had to buy back 50 million ounces of silver.

If they had to purchase back 100 million ounces of silver, the cost would skyrocket.

If they were to buy back all their net short positions, they would cannot obtain silver from COMEX because the exchange only possesses 102 million ounces.

With the COMEX vaults empty, the ETF purchasing more silver every day and a supply shortfall in the physical silver market, this would be the most bullish scenario ever for silver or any other commodity.

If you wish to profit from this likely scenario, I recommend investing in silver immediately and holding it for the long term. I do not anticipate the short position to begin unwinding for around another year. Still, after it occurs, silver demand will continue to exceed supply, resulting in a protracted bull market.

CHAPTER FOUR:
HOW DOES MONEY MOVE?

Capital

Capital is often cash or liquid assets being retained or obtained for expenditures. Examples:\s are Finance, Human Capital, Equity, Social capital, Debt capital, Working capital, Intellectual capital, Trade, Cultural capital, Natural capital, Economic capital, and Fixed capital.

There are many variations between dealing with angel investors and working with venture capital firms regarding the funding you need for your business.

There are major risks when undertaking an SBA loan since you will need to give a personal guarantee for the debt funding if you opt not to employ equity financing for your firm. Hard money may be an alternative for you to acquire money from outside funding sources for big tangible asset purchases.

You should first assess whether or not your business is deemed a small business per the definitions outlined by the Small Business Industry. A service and retail industry business would be considered modest provided its annual sales do not exceed $6 - $24.5 million, depending on the specific industry.

Angel investors want to engage with already profitable businesses as the risks are much fewer than a start-up business. Outside investment can aggressively and fast deliver growth in your firm if you require funds to boost your inventory, working capital or marketing.

Entrepreneurship must be treated as a career, and it should be underlined. To maintain profitability and good cash flow, a business must provide an improved product or service at a lower price than what is already available.

When constructing your forward-looking financial model, you should describe the business' valuation year-to-year basis so that a potential private funding source may comprehend the return on their investment.

When building a company plan specifically for a private funding source, it is important to adopt a broad perspective when promoting.

You should keep this in mind when seeking angel investors or other forms of external financing. If you're not seeking a business loan, you should know the complexities of small business finance.

In conclusion, you must consider the type of capital that makes the most sense for your organization. There are many ways to raise the necessary financing without giving up an excessive amount of stock in your organization.

If you have good credit, collateral and the ability to generate a positive cash flow, it may be in your best interest to seek a business loan before approaching private investors.
.

Leverage

This is a trading mechanism allows investors to increase their exposure to the market by paying less than the full investment amount.

Therefore, employing leverage in a stock transaction permits a trader to acquire a larger stock position without paying the full purchase price.

The concept of leverage is difficult for many novice traders to grasp. As a tool, leverage is extremely potent and can skyrocket your income but if done improperly, you could wind up amputating your foot!

HAVE YOU MET MONEY?

Many traders interchange the phrases margin and leverage. Margin and leverage are two completely distinct concepts that cannot be used together.

The general definition of leverage is "the mechanical advantage achieved by employing a lever." Remember that this definition is very accurate and in Forex words we can state that leverage, as defined by freedictionary.com, is as follows:

"The use of credit or borrowed funds to raise one's speculative capacity and the rate of return on an investment, such as when purchasing securities on margin."

Margin can be defined as follows:

The amount of collateral a consumer deposits when borrowing from a broker to purchase securities.

You use your account's deposit in foreign exchange to borrow from your broker to trade. This also implies that you cannot borrow unreasonable money. The Broker would have computed your risk position relative to his, resulting in ratios such as 1:100 or 1:500.

Which means you can borrow up to $500 with your $1 margin to trade FX. A normal person cannot possibly use all of his resources to trade on the Forex market without such borrowing.

There are risks associated with excessive leverage and what is known as a margin call. A margin call occurs when the funds in your account are inadequate to maintain your position. This indicates that you have lost so much money that, to preserve his interests, your broker has closed all of your positions.

A margin call indicates weak financial management skills. You should never be in such a predicament, as you have begun trading successfully by risking little more than 5 percent of your money. Greed destroys a business account very quickly. Overleverage and margin calls are two major tradings no- no's!

Therefore, leverage is what you borrow from your broker to trade. While Margin is used to finance your deal. You own the margin; it is your money.

Leverage is the broker's money; if you lose it, you will have to pay it back with your funds. They accomplish this by closing your position and taking your entire profit from the trade.

Consider utilizing $1,000 to control $100,000; leverage is a very effective technique. If you began trading without leverage, you could only go as high as $1,000. With leverage, you can accomplish a hundred times as much

Liquidity

This is the ease or speed with which a security can be bought or sold on the secondary market. When cash is needed, liquid investments can be sold quickly and without a large commission.

Liquidity is how quickly and easily an asset may be changed into cash. It is computed by evaluating three attributes of the asset:

- The rate at which an asset can be sold

- The number of times an asset can be sold

- What percentage of the asset's worth is lost when sold?

A liquid asset may be traded quickly and at nearly any moment without suffering significant loss.
The Imperative of Liquidity

Why is liquidity such a crucial idea for investors? Liquidity measures the ease with which an investor can enter and exit a market. In some respects, liquidity is similar to demand but not identical.

An asset with high, consistent and long-lasting demand is likely to have high liquidity, as potential purchasers are always available and typically prepared to pay a premium to acquire it.

By purchasing highly liquid assets, an investor retains the opportunity to convert his holdings to cash at any time - either to cut losses or walk away with a substantial profit.

In addition, it gives a safety net for investors who may have other financial obligations by granting them immediate access to their invested cash.

Patterns

Like every other market, the stock market is driven by the forces of demand and supply. Consequently, it experiences periodic ups and downs. The movement of the stock market determines the profitability of buying or selling a stock for an investor.

A market that has risen and achieved its peak will not be able to maintain its position at the apex indefinitely and will eventually decline. Similarly, once it reaches its lowest point, it will resurrect. This is the common consensus.

Since stock trade is based on stock price fluctuations and it is nearly difficult to foresee the market's future direction, trading stocks is risky.

For years, the objective of stock traders has been to forecast the behavior of the stock market as precisely as possible to maximize their profits by timing their entry and departure. Future analysts and researchers have attempted to uncover a pattern in the price movement to predict the market.

Because stock market moves are sometimes highly rapid and dramatic and other times quite stable, systematic and long-lasting, it is difficult to identify a consistent trend. To have a smooth pricing pattern, the time duration should be larger, as patterns with shorter time frames appear choppy and inconsistent.

The regular ups and downs of the stock market are influenced by many social, economic and political factors. Inflation, earnings, interest rates, political disturbances, fraudulent practices, increasing oil and energy costs, war and other political disturbances and uncertainty are known to create significant market volatility.

Since most market-moving forces are unpredictable, stock price fluctuations are similarly random. Diverse unanticipated economic news or events destabilize the market, which may result in severe financial depression.

On the other hand, favorable news may have the opposite impact, driving prices over expectations. Consequently, it is believed that discovering a pattern in these random market fluctuations can be somewhat challenging.

Stock market patterns are incomprehensible and convoluted. Indeed, the development of highs and lows follows a predetermined pattern and occurs cyclically.

There is order within the apparent disorder of bulls and bears. Those who cannot properly examine these patterns and comprehend the underlying rule cannot benefit from them.

After years of analyzing the financial markets, analysts have identified specific patterns that they believe can be used to accurately anticipate when and in what direction a market change will occur and future market crashes. However, they are unable to avert them.

Frequently, stock markets defy all laws and are notorious for their unpredictability and lack of discernible patterns. Contrary to forecasts, the stock market's bear or bull phases can frequently last for extraordinarily extended durations.

For instance, the bull market that ended in 2000 lasted as long as nine years. Therefore, rather than attempting to identify stock market patterns and take investment cues from them, it would be prudent to think long-term and design a robust portfolio with maximum returns regardless of randomness.

Bears

A bear market is a term used to describe a downward trend in the market. This is a condition characterized by declining securities and widespread pessimism. Investors are pessimistic about the markets and continue to sell, causing the market to decline further.

This increases pessimism and loss aversion, causing additional investors to sell, thereby creating a vicious cycle. There is no precise or agreed-upon definition of a bear market but a decline of 20% or more over two months is generally accepted.

Any number of factors can trigger a Bear market. Reduced consumer spending results from unemployment, the banking crisis, the absence of economic growth and the lack economic expansion.

It could be triggered by any event that causes investors and the general public to lose faith in the market, as investors begin selling equities out of fear of loss.

There have been many Bear markets throughout the years. In 1929, for instance, the Dow Jones industrial average fell from a peak of 381 on September 3 to a low of 199 on November 13. The Dow recovered 48% of its lost value in the subsequent five months.

This encouraged investors to re-enter the market in what would become a sucker rally. The market bottomed out on April 30, 1930 and in the subsequent 27 months, the Dow dropped by 86%.

Another instance occurred between 1973 and 1982. It began with the oil crisis and extended through the 1980s era of high unemployment.

Bear markets are advantageous for investors seeking to purchase equities at reduced prices for long-term holding or until the market recovers. Look for organizations with a stable financial history that will be around for the next decade.

If a company's share price has decreased owing to investors selling shares rather than constant financial losses, it may be an excellent investment. Companies continue to do business and generate profits during bad markets.

Money is to be made in every condition, including investing in a Bear market. There will be chances for the astute investor who diversifies his portfolio across many asset classes, such as options, equities and bonds.

Bulls

A "Bull Market" is characterized by rising investor statistics, confidence and motivation and all other market elements that entice investors to purchase a particular company in anticipation of a price increase soon.

The greatest market participants, who, when purchasing, induce a buying frenzy, is frequently referred to symbolically as the "Herd," presumably because they follow each other like bulls.

A 'Bull Market' may also be referred to as a bull run, about the characteristic behavior of bulls. The 'Dow Theory' explains the attitude of investors and the situation of the market in such circumstances.

The economy of the United States is constantly in flux, which causes the price to fluctuate as well. Many variables impact, control and determine the market.

Market manipulation is influenced by the supply and demand cycle, the behavior of the American populace, stock market interests and Federal Reserve interest rate fluctuations.

Occasionally, these elements provide a favorable environment for the market's growth over an extended period.

Thus, the financial world proclaims the arrival of a 'Bull Market,' When an investor considers how to spend in such a period of economic expansion, the age-old maxim "Buy low and sell high" comes to mind. Bullish investors look for offers, stocks, options or currencies that they believe will yield large profits.

They purchase this stock when they believe it is low and sell it when it is high. This proved fertile ground for some novice investors in this financial sector.

It is the bullish investors who believe the price will continue to rise, while a persistent downward flow of price characterizes the bear market.

Although history is somewhat sardonic towards the hypothesis, it is like a bull to assault its prey with its horns and thrust them upwards, possibly similar to the temptation of a stock market rise.

The earlier tournaments also featured a battle between the Bull and the Bear, which may explain the paradoxical terms of such offers.

Before investing, it is crucial to comprehend the trends and notions of a bull market; it is crucial to understand the rules before investing. Any investor must accept quality expenditures as a given but let's not forget that the fruit of long-term investments is also sweet.

Investment Instruments

The following is an explanation of the many investment options available to individuals. These explanations are based on my experience with them.

I. Funds

These funds are typically managed by an individual, fund manager, group, bank or organization. The company combines modest investment tranches to create a large pool of capital worth tens of millions of pesos. The funds are subsequently invested in the extremely volatile stock market. This investment is interesting for folks in their twenties and thirties.

How small is one tranche, then?

Typically, these organizations need a minimum investment of 25,000 and 50,000 Pesos. BPI meets the minimum investment requirement of $50,000.

Why would you combine them?

HAVE YOU MET MONEY?

There are two reasons for combining funds. First, you must meet the minimum purchase requirement to purchase stocks or equities on the stock market.

Occasionally, these minimum quantities approach 10,000 Pesos for a single item. Your 50,000 Pesos will not be exposed to all the good stocks and if you're unlucky, you may have purchased a stock whose price will plummet dramatically.

Second rationale:

With the pooled funds, the institution can hire expert portfolio managers with extensive experience. They are the industry's insiders. They are familiar with the stock price movement and the expected effects of good and bad news.

Occasionally, they may also have access to confidential information that can assist the management in selecting the best stock to purchase. Here, at least, the costly compensation of the managers is distributed among hundreds of investors.

A portfolio is a collection of stocks that a person monitors or invests in.

Illegal is insider trading based on privileged information. This privileged knowledge is so useful that it undoubtedly influences an investor's decision to purchase or sell a certain stock. Martha Stewart did this and made millions of dollars but she was caught, fined and sentenced.

What is the stock market's volatility?
The stock exchange is highly volatile. With 50,000 Pesos, it is possible to earn or lose 4,000 Pesos within three hours.

Is there a return guarantee?

NO. This is not a deposit to a bank. You can make money or lose it. Simply learn when to redeem and when to reinvest in the fund. It all comes down to time. Buy when the market is falling and sell when it is rising.

ii. Equity, balanced, bond, and mutual funds comprise the second category.

These are distinct categories of funds. Investments in the stock market are known as equity funds. Balanced funds consist of investments in government securities and stocks. Bond funds are investments in funds dedicated to government bonds and other bonds.

Typically, these funds are managed by private companies. The SEC supervises these funds administered privately.

III. Unit Investment Trust Funds (UITF)

This is a Fund-like entity. This is overseen by the Bangko Sentral ng Pilipinas and handled only by banks. The Bangko Sentral introduced worldwide standards for money management three years ago. Previously, it was the responsibility of the bank's portfolio managers to systematize their investing.

UITFs were previously known as common trust funds (CTF).

IV. Bonds

Bonds are institution-issued loans. Typically, bonds run from six months to many years. Governments and large corporations issue these bonds to generate funds. They will pay interest during the term of the bond. Typically, returns here exceed bank deposits.

Individuals typically do not have direct access to the bond market. Bond offerings are valued at tens of millions of Pesos, which is beyond the means of small investors. UITFs or Funds are how this can be accessed.

v. Treasury obligations

Treasury bills function similarly to bonds but have a shorter maturity. They range from three to twelve months. The returns are lower compared to bonds but superior to bank savings.

Again, UITFs and Funds are the simplest way to invest in Treasury Bills. Treasury bills are worth tens of millions of Pesos and are typically sold wholesale by the government.

The Bangko Sentral does, however, occasionally offer Retail Treasury Bills (RTB) at 5,000 Pesos each. You must seek particular institutions that sell these RTBs. Not all banks provide this product.

Equities

You may have recently heard a lot about home equity and home equity loans but if you're like most people, you can not completely understand what equity is or how it is used for loans and other purposes.

To assist you in understanding how equity works and how to utilize best the equity you have, a practical explanation of equity and its most popular applications are provided below.

Also, folks who do not have as much equity in their house or real estate as they would want are given information on how to increase equity.

What exactly is it?

If you're going to employ the equity you've accumulated, it's crucial that you fully comprehend what equity is and how it's utilized.

Equity is a measurement of how much of a mortgage loan has been repaid and how much of the property in the issue you "own." Typically, equity is expressed as a percentage, reflecting how much of the property's overall value you've contributed to its purchase.

Lenders can utilize the equity you've built up in your home or another real estate as collateral for low-interest loans or credit lines, creating a secondary lien on the property with its terms and rates distinct from the original mortgage.

Normal usage

The most typical application of equity is as collateral to get a loan. Due to the relatively high value of the most real estate and equity, many banks and other lenders are more than prepared to give reasonable interest rates on home equity loans, even to borrowers with less-than-perfect credit.

Depending on the lender, the value of the property, the amount of equity the borrower has in the property and the borrower's credit history, these home equity loans may be for a larger amount than the individual would otherwise be able to borrow.

Alternatives to traditional finance, continuing education, debt consolidation, home repairs and improvements and vacation planning are common uses of home equity loans.
Credit-based lines of credit

The other frequent application of equity is collateral for a line of credit. Similar to a home equity loan, different banks and other lenders may offer these credit lines to customers with varying credit scores.

Home equity lines of credit may even be given cheaper interest rates than some equity loans, as the borrowed amount is amortized over a longer period.

In place of a regular credit card or other credit line, equity lines of credit are frequently utilized in home renovation projects to pay for materials and labor and in various other personal and business endeavors.

The quantity of credit available on the credit line is influenced by some of the same variables that influence decisions regarding equity loans.

Mortgage payments

To increase the equity in your house or other real estates, it is essential to remain current on your mortgage payments and pay as much as possible toward the remaining balance. As you make mortgage payments, your equity will continue to increase.

If you take out a line of credit or loan using your home's equity, the amount borrowed will be added to the amount owed on your mortgage and will lower your equity, meaning you will also have to repay it to develop equity.

Fort knox

All institutions with a high level of security and restricted access become the topic of different conspiracy theories and works of fiction.

Area 51 is one of these enigmatic locations. Everyone believes that the United States Government uses this facility to study extraterrestrial life and time travel. Fort Knox is another structure that arouses the public's interest and inspires imagination.

Fort Knox is an alternative name for the U.S. Bullion Depository. It is a fortified vault where a significant portion of the United States gold reserves is stored. However, it holds a smaller quantity of gold than the New York Federal Reserve Bank.

The United States Mint also housed gold reserves in the Denver Mint, Philadelphia Mint, the West Point Bullion Depository and the San Francisco Assay Office addition to these two facilities.

The American people have stored gold and other culturally and historically significant artifacts, such as the English Crown Jewels and the Magna Carta, in Fort Knox.

During times of war, the Declaration of Independence and the Constitution of the United States were also put in the repository for preservation.
The 22-ton entrance of Fort Knox's granite fortification is sufficient to discourage any effort to breach its defenses. A complete army equipped with cutting-edge combat technology is prepared to act at the first sign of danger.

Fort Knox reportedly houses approximately 4,603 tons of gold bullion. The quantity of gold comprises gold bars, gold coin bars and gold coins. There are claims that the vault currently protects a smaller quantity of gold since it has been sold for other economic uses.

This is one of the many conspiracy theories that are impossible to substantiate because of the restricted public access to the Depository, despite the president's promises of improved transparency.

Gold has historically been an enticing temptation. After purchasing gold bullion, it is quite difficult to safeguard it. Since the security at

Fort Knox consists of alarms, video cameras, specially trained police officers and Army units, it is reasonable to assume that the United States Bullion Depository contains a substantial quantity of gold that can guarantee the nation's economic strength.

Inflation

Inflation is a persistent increase in prices, which causes a decline in the earnings and savings of the population. Even moderate inflation threatens the growth of the modern monetary economy. For this reason, all nations (including the most developed) implement anti-inflationary measures to lower inflation rates.

What reasons?

Inflation is a monetary phenomenon characterized by the issuance of excessive money relative to the supply of goods. This growth in wealth is due to different factors.

The first of these is the rise in population incomes that is not supported by a matching rise in the production of products. This increased demand boosts prices and the pace of inflation.

This imbalance between the supply and demand for products and services may also result from crop failures, import restrictions or monopolists' acts. Also, growing production costs and rising business expenses for employees, taxes and interest payments add significantly to inflation rate growth.

Moreover, the increase in prices for imported components indicates both a rise in global pricing and a decline in the value of the national currency. The weakening of the national currency can directly impact the prices of imported goods.

The overall impact of exchange rate fluctuations on price dynamics is referred to as the "transfer effect" and is often considered a separate inflation driver. The so-called "waiting moments" play a crucial part in the progression of the inflationary process.

The anticipated increase in pricing compels the populace to purchase items. Thus, a shortfall is generated for some of them, resulting in increased prices. It is challenging to reduce such inflationary assumptions.

Inflation can manifest in many ways. In a controlled economy (such as existed in the Soviet Union) and during wartime, when prices are fixed, inflation can have a concealed nature, referred to as suppressed inflation. It is followed by a shortage of various products, an increase in shadow trade, a dramatic rise in market prices, etc.

Nevertheless, rejecting such restriction (after the war or in nations that have transitioned from an administratively controlled to a market economy) often results in "galloping inflation" with a frenetic price increase. It results from the disparity between the quantity of money and the number of products.

The additional types of inflation include:

- Administrative inflation - inflation caused by "administratively" administered prices
- Galloping inflation - inflation manifesting as a spasmodic price surge;

- Hyperinflation - inflation with a very rapid price increase rate;

- Built-in Inflation is characterized by its average amount over a specific period.

- Imported inflation - inflation produced by external forces, such as an excessive influx of foreign currency into the country and an increase in import costs

-Induced inflation - inflation resulting from the effect of economic or external sources;

- Credit inflation - inflation induced by an excessive increase in credit

- Unanticipated inflation - the rate of inflation that has exceeded expectations for a certain period.

- Expected inflation - the estimated inflation rate in a future period due to current circumstances.

- Open inflation - inflation resulting from an increase in the cost of consumer products and producing resources

Hyper-Inflation

Hyperinflation is a high inflationary environment accompanied by soaring prices for goods and services and excessive currency devaluation.

When a currency is created without the requisite backing of a product, there will be an excess of money on the market, resulting in an imbalance between supply and demand.

Due to an abundance of money and a scarcity of commodities, prices of goods will surge. The greater the amount, the greater the potential for inflation to spiral out of control and become "Hyperinflation."

Over human history, over thirty nations have experienced hyperinflation and witnessed the devaluation of their currency. Germany in 1923, Greece in 1944, Hungary in 1946 and Taiwan in 1949 are just a few worst-case scenarios.

Hyperinflation is typically accompanied by a complete loss of confidence in the currency and will destroy the purchasing power of private and public savings. Furthermore, hyperinflation encourages overconsumption and the hoarding of real assets, making the affected nation unattractive to investors.

To illustrate the severity of hyper-inflation, consider the recent example of Zimbabwe, where a $100 billion banknote could only be used to purchase three eggs at the time it was created.

Well, it's no secret that following the 2008 market crisis, the U.S. government printed trillions of dollars to support its stimulus plans and bailouts, which will undoubtedly have repercussions.

Soon, all wealth and savings in the United States could be completely wiped out. We rapidly reach a run on the dollar, prompting a stampede toward gold and silver.

Unfortunately, by the time the typical American learns the truth, Gold prices will certainly exceed $5,000 per ounce and Silver prices will exceed $300 per ounce, making it impossible for them to preserve their purchasing power.

Stagflation

The phrase stagflation is a portmanteau of "economic stagnation" and "inflation," two economic phenomena once believed to be in opposition.

Economic stagnation is a prolonged period of sub-2 or sub-3 percent annual economic growth. On the other hand, inflation in this context refers to the fast devaluation of the currency.

Inflation reduces the currency's purchasing power, requiring ever-increasing sums to purchase products. During the interwar years in Germany's Weimar Republic, it took a wheelbarrow full of

Deutschmarks to purchase a loaf of bread. This is one of the most well-known instances of inflation.

This economic state is characterized by high unemployment and high inflation. Simply put, prices are rising rapidly while incomes remain constant.

A stagflation-afflicted economy effectively stagnates while profits are eroded by inflation. This may occur in countries with a weak currency that imports important products, such as food, where additional borrowing devalues their currency.

Most of the population becomes poorer due to inflation eroding their purchasing power. The primary threat of stagflation is that the economy has reached its lowest point but is stagnating. Like terminally ill patient who is slowly dying, their health deteriorates gradually as inflation sets in.

Compared to the state of the economy at the end of 2008, many economists may concur that stagflation indicates the economy has stopped declining.

However, stagflation ensues despite spending trillions of dollars on a "stimulus" package. To avert years of decline and further impoverishment of citizens, it may be necessary to implement new stimulus packages.

Most conventional economic strategies have been utilized to revive the economy. Due to the failure of tried-and-true economic solutions in the past, we may need to create new economic solutions. The United States escaped a cycle of stagflation in the 1970s by using "voodoo" economics under the Reagan administration.

Most governments have already decreased interest rates to all-time lows, reduced taxes and are lowering government spending, except for "New Deal"-related initiatives.

Governments, particularly the U.S., have already borrowed excessively and had the third-highest debt-to-GDP ratio, leaving less room for borrowing than before February 2009, which may need an increase in taxes rather than a decrease.

If Economists are correct, then the economic decline has been paused and our governments may need to find alternative ways to find trillions of dollars more to halt a continuous economic decline truly. Otherwise, we would experience a growing loss of wealth due to inflation and rising prices and be on the path to destruction.

Deflation

Deflation is a broad fall in prices for goods and services, generally accompanied by a contraction in the economy's supply of money and credit.

In academic terminology, deflation results from a decline in goods and services prices, typically during a recession. However, in the business world, it is customary for the prices of some new products, such as computers and electronics, to reduce gradually over time.

Japan comes to mind when we think about deflation in modern times. As Japan experienced a severe recession in the early 1990s, the nation's banks offered zero percent interest rates.

This encouraged savers to spend, while the suffering economy caused the basic price of many products and services to fall, increasing the purchasing power of cash-rich consumers and decreasing the wealth of debtors.

The decline in property values is an example of deflation in many economies, placing many banks in a paradoxical position. Many of these banking organizations have creditors who now owe more than their property was "worth" when they initially took out a loan on it - this is the liquidity trap.

Governments loathe deflation as much as they fear inflation because it lowers prices and living costs but at the same time punishes creditors who purchased at the old price and are still paying off their debt.

A nation's monetary policy is also affected by deflation, which cannot be stabilized due to the liquidity trap. It also transfers wealth from debtors and holders of deflated assets to holders of capital and currency. In 2010, while many people struggled with debt, the fraction of wealthy individuals in some economies grew wealthier.

Another negative effect of deflation is that it punishes individuals caught in the liquidity trap and has a trickle-up effect on the economy's wealth, as opposed to a trickle-down one.

It causes issues with the money supply and societal issues in more liberal economies. Greece is an example of how deflation on some goods - such as businesses and real estate - has sparked a "us versus them" mentality towards the growing wealthy elite.

Depending on their financial situation, some individuals appreciate deflation, while others suffer from the instability it produces.

While many products become more affordable, the wealth disparity in many nations widens, causing economic instability and economic stagnation. One reason why most economists concur is that fighting deflation is as vital as fighting inflation.

Depreciation

Depreciation is the decline in value of an asset over time, caused primarily by wear and tear. Depreciation is an essential component of every financial statement. Depreciation is the business practice of allocating an asset's cost over its useful life.

For tax purposes, businesses can deduct the cost of physical assets they acquire as business costs; however, they must depreciate these assets following IRS guidelines on how and when the deduction may be used dependent on the type of asset and the asset's useful life.

Accounting uses depreciation to attempt to match the expense of an asset with the income it generates for the business. Examples of depreciable objects include buildings, machinery, equipment, computers, outdoor lighting, parking lots, automobiles and trucks.

A portion of these assets' costs is consumed during each accounting period.

On the revenue statement, the portion being consumed is represented as "Depreciation Expense." During each year of an asset's life, depreciation is the transfer of a portion of the asset's cost from the balance sheet to the income statement.

Two accounting principles can be used to calculate and report depreciation: the cost principle and the matching principle.

According to the cost principle, the "Depreciation Expense" reported on the income statement and the asset amount recorded on the balance sheet must be based on the asset's original cost.

The matching principle stipulates that the asset's cost must be assigned to "Depreciation Expense" over its expected useful life.

This means that a portion of the asset's cost is reported on each income statement over the asset's useful life. By allocating a component of the asset's cost to various income statements, the accountant associates a piece of the asset's cost with each period used.

There are many types of depreciation: straight-line, sum-of-year-numbers, double-declining balance and modified accelerated cost recovery scheme (MACRS).

The straight-line depreciation technique is calculated by dividing the acquisition price of an asset by its salvage value by the number of years the asset may realistically benefit the firm. The straight-line technique equitably distributes the cost of an item across its useful life.

The Sum of the Year's Digits approach leads to a faster write-off than the straight-line method but is not as rapid as the declining balance method. Under the Sum-of-the-year's-digits technique annual depreciation is calculated by multiplying the Depreciable Cost by a fractional schedule.

The double-declining technique of depreciation is slightly more sophisticated than the straight-line method since it doubles the amount of depreciation in the first year. After the first year, the same percentage is multiplied by the remaining balance to be depreciated in consecutive years. After the Tax Reform Act of 1986, the MACRS method of depreciation was introduced.

This approach permits greater accelerated depreciation of assets over a longer period. Profitable businesses commonly use this strategy since it helps them to pay off assets faster. MACRS has no salvage value; instead, it uses annual schedules to depreciate assets to zero.

Erosion

This includes any adverse effect on a company's assets or money. Profits, sales and tangible assets such as manufacturing equipment are susceptible to deterioration.

Erosion is often regarded as a general risk factor inside a company's cash management system, as losses can gradually occur over time. As time passes, the value of some financial assets, such as options contracts and warrants, can erode, a phenomenon known as time decay.

In the United States, we have a concept known as the American Dream; part of it is opportunity. When individuals attempt to portray as villains those who have successfully garnered support for high taxes, they appear to lose sight of this fact.

It is possible for anyone, including an immigrant, to accumulate money in our country. The Emma Lazarus poem "The New Colossus," inscribed on a plaque near the Statue of Liberty, says it all: "Give me you're tired, your destitute yearning to breathe free,

The wretched refuse of your teeming shore." Send these destitute, storm-tossed individuals to me as I raise my torch beside the golden entrance!

In part, the American Dream centers around the potential to amass wealth; yet, when you succeed, the inheritance tax is there to take it away.

When you honestly examine the 35 percent tax rate without taking into account the recent reduction and applying it to your legacy across multiple generations, the consequences are shocking.

Depending on the size of your estate, this rate permits the government to take approximately half of your bequest over two generations.

Do nothing to protect your assets. The Internal Revenue Service will eventually acquire them all, leaving your descendants with only the exempt fraction of your original legacy to work with.

You may construct a generation-skipping trust to safeguard at least a portion of your hard-earned riches. With these instruments, you identify your grandchildren as beneficiaries rather than your children.

However, your children can still get dividends from the trust and use the property in it, even though they do not own the assets.

Your grandkids will inherit the assets upon their demise and although both generations benefited from the trust, there will be only one estate tax to pay.

Volatility

Volatility in finance is the statistical measurement of asset price movements across time. If an asset's price fluctuates rapidly and dramatically, its volatility will be significant.

If prices are stable and rarely fluctuate, then price volatility is low. Volatility is measured by the standard deviation annualized.

Volatility as a Risk Metric

Volatility is often employed as a risk metric. Many standard risk metrics, such as beta, incorporate volatility into their calculations. It makes it obvious that an asset with large price fluctuations is riskier than one with low volatility.

Upside Volatility vs. Downside Volatility

However, the efficiency of employing volatility as a risk indicator is dubious. The primary flaw of volatility is that it does not distinguish between upward and downward price swings. For example, suppose the stock price fell from $10 to $2.

Also suppose that the stock's volatility was minimal before this price decline. In this instance, volatility was lower when the share price was $10 than when it was $2.

If volatility had been employed as a measure of risk in this example, the stock would have been less dangerous when it was valued at $10. This hypothesis is illogical.

Predictions' Limitations

In addition, volatility is a time-based assessment dependent on historical data. However, past events may not predict future outcomes.

Using historical volatility as a predictor of future risk is therefore constrained by the unpredictability of future returns. The financial markets are characterized by abundant unexpected future returns and extreme events.

Despite flaws, evaluating risks using volatility is a crucial component of risk management; nonetheless, the forecasting limits of the measurements must be taken into account.

Alerts vs signals vs triggers

When novice traders enter the index futures market, creating a successful method is one of their initial priorities. Although market approach systems consist of many modules, emini alerts are among the most essential.
How can a trader do profitable executions if he is unaware of market conditions? Nonetheless, a system with too many "bells and whistles" can render a trader ineffective due to information overload. When trading index futures, simplicity is typically the optimal strategy.

HAVE YOU MET MONEY?

As a trader, you are daily inundated with information from every conceivable source. All factors, including financial reports, upgrades, downgrades, wire services and geopolitical developments, influence the financial markets.

With all these possible distractions, it is crucial to filter the amount of information we process while monitoring the futures market. This is where emini alerts and signals may help us maintain our concentration.

A successful emini trading system will provide you with these notifications, notifying you when entry possibilities are available. They sift through market noise, dynamics and internals to provide you with the essential data you need to make intelligent entry and exit decisions.

By utilizing alerts, you can reduce the likelihood of poor executions. The trading system will send valid signals, motivating you to execute trades with a high proportion of successful executions upon entry and exit.

You can develop trading systems with built-in emini alerts or purchase systems designed by seasoned futures traders using their trading approach as the system's foundation.

Some use traditional Japanese candlestick patterns, while others utilize pivot points around key support and resistance zones. Others will employ micro-fast emini scalp trading, pocketing little profits throughout the daily session.

Whether you engage in day trading or scalp trading on the index futures market, emini alerts should be an integral component of your trading system.

Not only will they help you eliminate unnecessary data but they will also assist you to identify successful trading opportunities.

Chapter Five:
How do I use money?

Infinite Returns

Over the past few years, I've observed that many individuals have unreasonable expectations regarding the returns on their investments.

HAVE YOU MET MONEY?

In this section, I'll address some factors that could impact your potential return and we'll examine what realistic returns you could expect based on the type of portfolio you have.

Why do returns fluctuate?

You can already be familiar with the notion of risk and return and realize that various investments offer different rates of return, typically based on the level of risk they entail. By mixing these various investments (diversification), you can smooth out your returns; different sectors will perform well at various times.

Some investments, such as stocks and real estate, are anticipated to outperform more cautious investments, such as cash, over the long term.

In the near term, stocks and real estate may occasionally experience weak years and the cash portion of your portfolio will mitigate your overall losses during these periods.

The more you invest in growth assets (shares and property), the greater the potential for larger returns over the long term, but you must be aware that negative returns may occur more frequently due to the higher risk and volatility of these investments. If you hold more cash and fixed-interest investments, your returns will be less volatile but lower over the long run.

Why is it important?

When we meet with you, we typically spend some time learning about your aims and goals. Then, we consider appropriate financial methods to assist you to attain your goals and objectives.

We examine your existing financial standing and compare it to your planned future. Then, we determine whether you are saving enough to reach your objectives. In these computations, the expected return is a critical factor.

If the predicted return is poor, you can need to invest more to reach your long-term objectives. If predicted returns are substantial, you can invest less.

Setting reasonable yields is crucial. If we exaggerate your predicted rate of return, we may give you false hope that you can attain your objectives.

Multiple options

We assist you in determining your risk tolerance and your portfolio's asset allocation. We utilize different portfolios with our clients. Conservative, moderate and growth economic policies are usually the most popular.

The Conservative portfolio features a greater allocation to cash and fixed interest and a smaller allocation to stocks and real estate. This portfolio is likely less volatile than the moderate and growth portfolios but will not generate the same long-term returns.

Long-term estimates for the portfolio of the Conservatives are 7.3% per year. It is 8.2% for the Moderate portfolio and 8.8% for the Growth portfolio.

These are merely calculated averages. On the surface, 8.8% may not appear to be a particularly great return for a portfolio that is 80% invested in growth assets.

The actual annual returns could be far greater (or lower). S&P predicts a 90% possibility that the Growth portfolio's annual return might range from -6% to +25.1% in any given year.

Thus, some years will be good while others will be disastrous. They anticipate that the long-term average will be approximately 8.8%.

HAVE YOU MET MONEY?

However, it is essential to note that past performance is not indicative of future performance.

Taking precautions is the prudent course

Long term, it is possible that these portfolios will outperform S&P's projections. However, they may not and if you are planning for your retirement, wouldn't you want to base your assumptions on conservative projections instead of predicted profits that may not materialize?

And if you are now in retirement, wouldn't it make more sense to choose a draw-down rate from your portfolio that assures you that your funds will last as long as possible?

What matters most?

This secret could be one of the most significant pieces of financial advice you ever get.

In the end, the projected rate of return is merely a number you will likely never attain.

I can guarantee that you will never receive the promised rate of return exactly. You can average higher or lower but I highly doubt you will ever reach that exact rate and it doesn't matter.

The projected return is useful for determining how much you must save for the future to have any chance of reaching your long-term goals. It serves as a good beginning point.

But what is incomparably more valuable is monitoring your progress toward your plan frequently. Your plans will inevitably evolve.

The date you intend to retire could change, as could the amount of income you desire in retirement, your contributions, the rate of inflation and the rate of return you receive.

By periodically monitoring your progress, you can make the small (or large) adjustments necessary to stay on course. By maintaining reasonable expectations on the levels of return you could attain, you lessen the chance of not having sufficient funds to cover your future lifestyle expenses.

Types of accounts

There are many types of checking accounts, most of which impose fees for deposits, withdrawals, inactivity and opening an account to make checks.

If feasible, always choose a free account but it is also vital to research the types of free accounts accessible to select one that meets your demands.

Most Credit Unions offer different free options. You can choose a free account that meets your demands because each account offers a unique set of advantages.

Standard Free Checking

Basic Free Checking Accounts are free and account balances accrue interest. There is a $25 minimum deposit required to open the account but there is no minimum balance after that.

This account may come with a complimentary Visa debit card and access to complimentary Rewards Programs. This will earn you awards simply for utilizing it routinely.

HAVE YOU MET MONEY?

This free checking account is an excellent alternative for consumers who are just starting or who do not maintain a large account balance.

Bonus Debit Checking

In addition, Bonus Debit Checking accounts are completely free and only need a minimum deposit of $25 to open. You will receive access to tens of thousands of surcharge-free ATMs. This account may reimburse you up to $10 for ATM costs incurred at a different financial institution.

In addition, as a member of your Credit Union, you will receive additional rewards points and periodic offers for unique bonus incentives, both of which will stretch your budget with benefits.

These accounts may also provide free mobile banking and mobile deposits and a free Visa debit card linked to your Rewards program, allowing you to collect rewards whenever you use the card.

Benefit Checking

These accounts are likewise free and a $25 minimum deposit is required to open one. You will receive the same benefits as Bonus Debit Checking account holders, plus increased interest payouts on the first $500 when you make at least six transactions. Also, the first box of checks is free upon account opening. Customers with larger balances will appreciate this, increasing their interest earnings.

If you are interested in getting a new checking account or perhaps upgrading to a free one, your local credit union has a checking account that suits your needs. In addition to a selection of free checking accounts, you can also have free internet access to check your balance simply.

Average Dollar costs

One of the holy grails of investing is earning a satisfactory return without experiencing volatility. Ultimately, I believe we have all learned that the shortest distance between two places is a straight line.

It is an understatement to think that we are far from attaining this objective, but dollar cost averaging can be useful until we reach this objective.

Simply put, dollar cost averaging entails investing at predetermined intervals over a predetermined period. Instead of investing a large sum at a single share price, dollar cost averaging invests when prices are both high and low, thereby averaging the share price.

There is a contention that dollar cost averaging (DCA) can reduce the return on investment and I do not disagree with this contention. If a buy is made while the share price is low and the price subsequently surges, the results will be better than if the purchase was made at a higher average price. Second, dollar cost averaging over a short period frequently does not allow the process enough time to reveal its true colors.

Thus, to properly benefit from dollar cost averaging, an investor must recognize that it is a long-term process that depends more on reduced volatility than on absolute return on investment.

When conducting investing research, examining returns over one, three and five years is beneficial. However, we must remember that they are simply "frozen" snapshots of investment returns at predetermined time intervals.

With dollar cost averaging, our demand for finances occurs not only after these intervals but also during the entire period. This gives validity to the ongoing requirement for reduced volatility.

Dollar-cost averaging can be an excellent method for investors who engage in asset allocation to rebalance a portfolio regularly.

Rather than buying and selling to rebalance, investing regularly (monthly, quarterly, etc.) can restore the asset allocation to the desired levels. This technique manages the tax burden on prospective gains by minimizing trading activity.

There is a strong possibility that you are already enrolled in a dollar-cost averaging program. Two good examples of dollar cost averaging are monthly 401(k) contributions and quarterly dividend reinvestment programs. In addition, mutual funds feature "systematic deposit" systems that regularly withdraw cash from checking or savings accounts regularly.

There is no assurance that dollar cost averaging will result in a profit. This technique does not protect against market losses. This method entails continuing investments in securities independent of market fluctuations.

Before implementing a dollar-cost-averaging technique, you should evaluate your ability to continue purchasing during periods of low prices.

Also, the method is not a replacement for investing research. Bad investments will always result in a loss, regardless of your technique. Consider dollar cost averaging if you are interested in long-term investing and wish to reduce your portfolio's volatility.

Portfolio

Portfolio management comprises activities that aid investors in attaining their financial goals. Profit maximization is the objective of portfolio management, which entails structuring and managing businesses and other organizations to achieve this end.

Portfolio management optimizes the use of personnel, capital, and other assets. In brief, it is the ability to optimize assets and increase the value of a portfolio.

The company's senior management team is solely responsible for portfolio management. Sometimes they are referred to as "product committees."

Portfolio management improves managers' grasp of a business's costs, risks and capabilities. The portfolio management effort must match the strategy of the corporate organization.

With the aid of performance measures, the result is evaluated. The two primary portfolio management types are enterprise and project portfolio management.

Enterprise portfolio management selects investments based on the enterprise architecture-determined business requirements and value. Project portfolio management offers a structured method for making portfolio-related choices.

The allocation of assets is a crucial component of any portfolio management approach. Allocation of assets determines the proportions of a portfolio's investments in various asset classes.

There are two types of asset allocation: active and passive. Active asset allocation relies on market perspectives.

Portfolio management is a potent tool for making deliberate decisions and estimating expenses. It also assists investment bankers in categorizing investments, such as blue chip stocks, mutual funds and bonds, into many groups.

An efficient portfolio management facilitates the expansion of businesses and other organizations. It facilitates the organization of necessary resources and maximizes revenue. The administration of a portfolio ties together activities, resources and policies.

Individual and institutional investors have access to many professional portfolio management programs. Using a comprehensive customer profile procedure, they assist the client in determining the optimal asset allocation and investment strategy.

Portfolio weighting

A portfolio is a collection of assets. Portfolio theory demonstrates how an investor might optimize his portfolio position. The portfolio theory is predicated on the premise that the investor's utility is a function of the mean return and the variance (or its square root, the standard deviation) of return.

Consequently, it is also known as the mean-variance portfolio theory or the two-parameter portfolio theory. It is assumed that the investor prefers a greater mean return over a lower one and a smaller variation of return over a higher one.

The expected return on a portfolio is just the weighted arithmetic mean of the expected returns of the portfolio's assets. The portfolio's rate of return standard deviation measures the portfolio's riskiness.

Any number of portfolios can be assembled from the investments accessible to an investor. Each feasible portfolio can be depicted on a two-dimensional graph based on its predicted rate of return and standard deviation of the rate of return.

The investor should select the investment portfolio that maximizes his utility function. This decision needs two steps: defining the set of efficient portfolios and selecting the optimal portfolio from that set. The efficient frontier is identical for all investors since the portfolio theory assumes that investors have identical expectations.

We have simply described what a set of efficient portfolios entails. How can this set be achieved from the many portfolio options available to the investor?

Graphical analysis, calculus analysis or quadratic programming analysis may be utilized to discover the set of efficient portfolios.

The primary benefit of graphical analysis is that it is simpler to comprehend. Graphical analysis cannot handle portfolios including more than three stocks.

Since n-dimensional space can be handled by mathematical analysis, the calculus technique can manage portfolios comprising any number of stocks.

The analysis of quadratic programming can also handle any number of securities and inequalities. The quadratic programming approach is the most useful approach for practical purposes.

Portfolio diversification

There are two categories of risk in financial markets: market risk (systematic risk) and firm-specific risk (specific risk). Note that the performance of your portfolio will depend more on the profitability of the market than on the returns of individual stocks.

Thus, having shared with great potential in your portfolio is less important than investing during market uptrends.

When purchasing shares in a publicly traded firm, you always risk the company going bankrupt, its revenues collapsing or even a factory catching fire.

On the other hand, the market as a whole will never fail and the aggregate total revenue has little possibility of falling. Portfolio diversification is the only method of mitigating specific risks.

HAVE YOU MET MONEY?

Having more lines in your portfolio will not prevent one of your assets from going bankrupt but the potential loss will be lesser in relative terms because more lines also mean less weight on each holding.

By maintaining a portfolio of 10 to 15 lines, you greatly reduce your specific risk in exchange for a systematic risk you cannot avoid. Take October 1987 as an example: regardless of industry affiliation, all equities experienced a significant decline.

Selection of stocks for portfolio managers

In selecting investments, most portfolio managers do not prioritize stocks that outperform the market but rather:

A collection of financial assets: An individual should behave similarly to a portfolio manager, even though the amounts involved are rarely the same. It is considerably simpler for the portfolio manager to invest in U.S. Treasury bills or Russian bonds than for an individual.

In this procedure, he determines the optimal distribution of his portfolio based on the type of the required investments (stocks, bonds, currency, real estate.). If he anticipates a decline in the stock market, he will increase the proportion of bonds in his portfolio.

A sample of industries: Once the asset allocation is determined (let's assume our portfolio is 60% invested in equities), the manager selects the market-beating sectors. He may select the oil, automobile, construction or technology industries.

These decisions are determined primarily by sector analyses conducted by financial professionals. Suppose our portfolio manager decides to invest 10 percent of his portfolio in the New Technology industry.

Location Selection: The geographical selection can be undertaken concurrently with the sector selection. It compels the manager to pick among various exchanges.

The globalization of financial markets is the globalization of the economy. Hundreds of billions can change countries in a matter of days. Therefore, the management can choose Wall Street, emerging markets, the Paris stock exchange or even Tokyo.

Individuals and portfolio managers devote most of their time to selecting securities but most of a portfolio's profitability is determined by the first three decisions.

The profitability of a portfolio is unrelated to the selection of stocks or their prices. Suppose our manager decided to invest 10% of his New Technology portfolio in "Yahoo," which would be 10% (Yahoo) x 10% (New Tech Industry) x 60% (Shares) = 0.6% of his whole portfolio.

Physical Portfolio

This section focuses primarily on real-asset investments and is intended to highlight some of the portfolio planning characteristics of physical assets when considered part of a well-diversified and balanced investment portfolio and some of the inherent risks to be considered when allocating investment capital to specific, niche investment sectors or projects.

Tangible asset values, lower volatility, and the possibility of greater investment performance that is not reliant on the performance of typical financial investments are just a few of the many advantages of hard or real assets.

However, when considering an investment in real or physical assets, prospective investors must take into account not only the risk of loss due to market fluctuations, but also the risk of loss due to operational or managerial risks unique to the asset class and, of course, counterparty risk exposure.

Portfolio Management Benefits

Every asset class exhibits different characteristics when viewed from the perspective of an Investor or Financial Planner and Investors invariably choose to invest in specific assets to achieve specific goals, such as risk mitigation, portfolio insurance, superior returns and hedging against inflation or other potential economic impacts on the value and performance of their portfolio.

Here, we examine some of the general portfolio planning characteristics associated with different alternative physical assets.

Capital Values

Investors deploy capital to hard assets to underwrite the value of their portfolio and protect against the danger of the values of listed financial assets falling dramatically at any given time.

In reality, many assets, such as gold, have a 'safe-haven' appeal, gaining value when stock markets collapse as investors sell stocks and purchase gold.

Independent Returns

The characteristics that sustain real-asset value growth and income are frequently dissimilar to the fundamentals that support traditional investments.

Typically, alternatives have a direct negative correlation with the performance of equities and bonds, allowing investors to balance their portfolios and profit when other portfolio components lose value or perform poorly. Occasionally, this method is referred to as portfolio insurance.

Diversification

Diversification, a crucial element of risk management in financial planning, spreads one's investment risk over different holdings, lowering the probability of holding too many "eggs in one basket."

Diversifying a portfolio's holdings across sectors and assets minimizes the chance that a single asset's poor performance would negatively affect the portfolio as a whole.

Inflation Protection

Many alternative investment assets exhibit a strong positive association with inflation, appreciating at a faster pace than the current inflation rate.

This effectively mitigates the impact of inflation on investment portfolios' real value. For this reason, pension funds, university endowments, insurance firms and other institutional investors purchase farmland and forestland as long-term investments.

Superior Returns

Many alternative investment assets have significantly outperformed traditional investment assets over the long term, as depicted in the graph below.

Although all sectors and methods contain inherent risk, it has been demonstrated that well-picked and well-managed real assets generate greater investment returns for investors who can tolerate short-term price swings and long-term investment perspectives.

When other income assets, such as cash deposits, underperform, operational assets, such as real estate, generate useful income.

No one knows the future

In 2004 and 2005, investors caught in the pre-construction bubble listened to advise that described booming conditions in some regions.

Consequently, thousands of eager speculators flooded the market just as savvier analysts were advising clients to get out of Las Vegas, Phoenix and South Florida.

The investors who survived the pre-construction bust exited the market at its peak, as it was evident from an analysis of market cycles that the economy would soon be in decline. What rises must also fall.

Nobody has a crystal ball so accurate that it eliminates all investment risk. No one could have foreseen the 2005 hurricane season, which resulted in construction delays in the summer of 2005 and massive construction cost increases in 2006, further delaying contracts signed a year or more prior.

Few pessimists predicted a total collapse of the housing market and it turned out that those who took a conservative approach to invest in real estate in 2004 and 2005 were the most successful.
Those caught in the housing massacre are frequently paralyzed by the fear of reentering the hunt. Focusing solely on the past is equally destructive as focusing solely on the present. Permit the past to inform your future but not to dictate your future actions.

Once again, the housing market is fraught with uncertainty. Will a double-dip recession occur?

Before a gradual reversal, will housing prices languish at rock-bottom levels for an extended time? Who knows definitively?

We can make projections based on the observed trends. Always have a backup exit strategy in place in case circumstances change.

A strategy of flipping short sales, REOs or other wholesale properties makes much sense in the current economic climate.

Even though prices are beginning to rise in some markets, many analysts anticipate widespread price declines or stagnation over the next couple of years.
Therefore, "buy and hold" properties purchased as rentals must justify themselves based on cash flow rather than rapid appreciation.

Currently, only cash-flowing properties should be purchased to hold. Everything else should be sold at attractive prices to those currently in a "buy and hold" position.

Most investors' best primary strategy is accumulating cash through short sales and other transactional deals. It permits the Investor to pay down debt and be in a strong position to withstand future economic downturns.

When the ultimate buy signal is generated, short sale investors will be in a great position to capitalize due to their substantial liquid assets and low debt-to-income ratio.

There are many ways to generate money in real estate but they are all ineffective unless you have a constant flow of motivated sellers and qualified buyers. When you have a robust pipeline of prospects, you can select the best of the best and finally take charge of your financial destiny.

Entry planning

HAVE YOU MET MONEY?

Even more crucial than your stock entry strategy is your stock exit strategy. You do not earn any money until you sell a stock. You can purchase at the optimal time but if you do not have a solid exit strategy, you can still lose money on the trade. Consider the following: purchasing a stock for $10 rises to $20 in three months. Did you profit? Well, it depends on whether you sold it or not.

You could still lose money if you did not sell it. If the stock price rises to $8 and you do not have a stop loss, you are now in the red. Because of this, it is important to know where you will exit.

Here are two strategies that most professional traders employ.

Having a destination and a goal

This is the system that probably most professional traders will employ. It is straightforward and devoid of emotion. You simply purchase a stock and determine your target using an indicator such as a chart pattern or the stock's true value.

Then, you place a stop on the stock that represents the maximum loss you are willing to accept for any given position. This is an excellent strategy because once you enter a trade, you cannot make decisions.

You simply dispose of the stock. If the price reaches your objective, you exit with a profit; if it reaches your stop, you exit with a small loss. It is straightforward and employs little emotion.

Exhibiting a trailing halt

This is an excellent technique since it entails purchasing or selling a stock with a stop loss. As the market continues to rise in your favor, you adjust your stop loss to retain a portion of your earnings even if the stock goes against you.

Eventually, as the stock rises and you raise your stop, you will be stopped out of your position, ideally with a profit.

Regardless of your stock exit strategy, you should know what to do before investing. Also, you should stick to one strategy. Stick to a single strategy and become an expert user of it to make money on the stock market.

Short term planning

Regardless of how volatile the markets may be, it is crucial to have a plan of action in place in the current era. Investors should not withdraw from the market but rather redistribute their funds according to a long-term and short-term plan.

The short-term plan should include stocks that are LEAST likely to experience issues. In addition to having a short-term plan, you should also be working toward a larger long-term plan.

Thus, a short-term plan could consist of investing solely in large-cap stocks with high dividend yields but reinvesting the dividends in small-cap stocks with higher risk.

Your long-term objective may be to invest in great small-cap companies when they are just starting out. Still, you are aware that it is extremely difficult to find such companies due to the state of the economy, so you buy large, stable companies and only risk the dividend income you receive.

The preceding example illustrates a short-term plan for navigating the current economic downturn while simultaneously working towards the investor's long-term goal and market strategy.

However, this doesn't imply that you should only adopt a long- and short-term strategy during a recession; rather, you should adopt a long- and short-term plan regardless of what is happening in the world.

There are many ways to create long-term and short-term plans based on the current state of the energy, housing, banking and economy.

Sometimes the best action is to invest a fixed amount of money each month, regardless of the circumstances. Suppose you can invest a certain amount of money each month in a certain number of diversified securities. In that case, you will almost certainly earn a profit because the stock market has always risen.

However, if you decide to create a long- and short-term investment strategy, there are some questions you must ask yourself. How much risk you are planning to take should be the first question you ask yourself.

If you can assume more risk, you must include this variable in your overall market analysis. How much money do you want to be able to retire on?

This is another important question individuals should ask themselves. If you want to retire with more money, you will need to take on more risk, as higher risk can result in higher returns.
If you have the skills to take calculated and reasonable risks, taking on more risks is not necessarily negative. Calculated risk and plan does not entail investing in seemingly inexpensive stocks at random but rather considering the market value of the company.

Market makers

One thing you should know about the Forex market is that within the inner circle of elite traders are individuals and institutions that can alter the market's direction and flow.

These individuals have access to unlimited funds and will spend them as they see appropriate, typically with their own and the market's best interests in mind.

One is governments, who view the Forex market as an opportunity to make more money and stabilize the economy by leveraging their currency reserves.

Governments have as much or more of a stake in the Forex market as the typical trader because their currency is the one that is represented in the trading environment.

Thus, they must defend and use as much of it as possible to strengthen their own. For one thing, governments trade in both directions.

First, they will use routine trading to make money, utilizing massive resources to generate gains and pips that retail traders can only imagine.

In addition, they trade in a way that protects the value of their respective currencies and prevents one from overpowering the other.

Inflation is a significant issue for the global economy and governments and they will utilize the Forex market to defend themselves from this phenomenon.

Therefore, governments with vast access to currency would often pump millions of dollars into the Forex market to attempt to influence price movements, with large central banks serving as their sole competition and balance maker.

These big edifice banks are truly present to invest their money in the Forex market and to ensure that those with access to large sums of money do not manipulate the market in an excessively directional manner.

They have a vested interest in the Forex market and the investing industry. The Forex market will only continue if there are investors there who are interested in making money.

Considering that retail investors are often helpless in the eyes and hands of market movers, governments and large central banks serve as checks and balances to ensure that everything goes according to plan.

On the Forex market, these are some market movers, although there are also smaller market movers, such as hedge fund authorities and even smaller banks. Because of the market's openness and fluidity, competition is fair and practically never biased.

As Forex trading is a market governed by checks and balances, even central banks and governments have little authority against the rush of a single market movement by millions of investors from all over the world if such an event were to occur.

Among the twelve LBMA market makers are the following banks: Citibank, Standard Chartered Bank, BNP Paribas, ICBC Standard Bank, Credit Suisse, Goldman Sachs, HSBC, JP Morgan Chase, Merrill Lynch, Morgan Stanley, TD Bank, UBS and Standard Bank of Canada

Feasibility study

A Feasibility Study is, in its simplest form, a characterization of the problem or opportunity to be explored, an analysis of the current mode of operation, a specification of the requirements, an evaluation of the alternatives and an agreed-upon path of action.

Consequently, the processes for creating a Feasibility Study are generic. They may be applied to any project, whether for systems and software development, making an acquisition or any other form of project.

There are essentially six components to any viable Feasibility Study:

1. The PROJECT SCOPE defines the business issue or opportunity to be handled. The proverb "A problem adequately articulated is half solved" is highly applicable. The Scope should be precise and concise; a narrative that wanders serves no purpose and might potentially mislead project participants.

It is also vital to identify the sectors of the business that will be directly or indirectly affected, including project participants and end-user areas. Identify the project's sponsor, especially if he or she is footing the money.

Too many corporate projects have been initiated without a well-defined Project Scope. As a result, projects have gone in and out of their boundaries, forcing them to produce either significantly more or less than what is required.

2. The CURRENT ANALYSIS is utilized to define and comprehend the current implementation approach, such as a system, a product, etc.

From this research, it is not uncommon to learn that the current system or product has nothing wrong with it other than certain misunderstandings or requiring minor adjustments instead of a complete redesign.

Also, the strengths and limitations of the existing strategy are identified (pros and cons). Also, there may be components of the present system or product that can be included in its replacement, saving time and money in the future. Without such examination, this may never be identified.

Analysts are urged against the temptation to halt the current system and fix any flaws identified at this time. Simply document your results; otherwise, you will waste unnecessary effort at this stage (aka "Analysis Paralysis").

3. REQUIREMENTS - How requirements are defined relies on the project's focus. For instance, how criteria for a product are described differs significantly from those for a building, a bridge or an information system.

Each is defined differently as a result of their distinct qualities. How requirements are defined for software differs significantly from how they are defined for systems. (See "Deciphering the Puzzle of Specifications")

4. The APPROACH is the suggested solution or action plan to meet the requirements. Here, different solutions are evaluated, explaining why the preferred approach was chosen.

To test the viability of design-related projects, entire rough designs (such as "renderings") are generated here. The usage of existing structures and commercial options are also investigated at this stage (e.g., "build versus buy" decisions). However, the most important concerns are:

* Does the suggested method meet the requirements?

* Is it also a viable and practical solution? (Will it be performed in Poughkeepsie?)

To complete the next step, a comprehensive analysis is required here.

5. EVALUATION - evaluates the cost-effectiveness of the selected Approach. This begins with a study of the project's expected total cost. To provide a cost comparison, additional alternatives are evaluated in addition to the preferred solution.

An estimate of labor and out-of-pocket expenses for development projects is compiled alongside a project schedule depicting the project's path and beginning and ending dates.

After calculating the project's entire cost, a cost and evaluation summary are compiled that contains a cost-benefit analysis, return on investment, etc.

ALL PARTIES CONDUCT A FORMAL REVIEW OF THE FEASIBILITY STUDY AFTER ALL PREVIOUS ELEMENTS HAVE BEEN COMPILED INTO IT.

The review has two purposes: to verify the completeness and quality of the Feasibility Study and to make a project decision; either approve, reject or request that it be altered before a final decision is made.

If the proposal is approved, all participants must sign the paper indicating their agreement and dedication to it; this may seem like a minor gesture but signatures carry a lot of weight as the project continues. If the Feasibility Study is denied, the reasons for its denial must be outlined and linked to the document.

Market price

This is the price an asset would fetch on the open market or the value the financial community places on a particular stock or company.

In market-based pricing, the only rational price to charge is what customers believe the product to be worth. Things sold at auction, such as on the art market, are obvious examples.

The price is as high as the highest bidder is willing to go. Similar restrictions apply to a considerable extent in the secondary property market, where sellers are free to set any price they like but must eventually negotiate the best price a buyer will pay.

In many instances, however, the consumers' opinion of the goods being offered is an essential factor. This can be the most important factor when the products are distinctive and/or appeal to a specific group of individuals.

Cost-Based Pricing

In a highly competitive environment, businesses may have the possibility to acquire customers if they can provide a low enough price. This is especially true when individual contracts are negotiated, as in the case of large construction projects. Still, it is also becoming increasingly apparent in markets such as those for electrical appliances, where electricity boards, discount stores and other large retail chains are often able to "shop around" for the best bulk discounts.

The question that may emerge is, "What is the lowest level at which it makes sense to operate?" One method for achieving this is to calculate marginal costs. The marginal cost in economics is the cost of producing one additional unit.

In most cases, this indicates that fixed expenses have already been repaid by adequate unit sales volume. The cost of creating additional units impacts just the variable costs. Therefore even if a very modest profit per unit may be added, the business is still profitable.

We can then argue that even if there were no profit, the firm would still be worthwhile since it may utilize resources (including people) that would otherwise be idle. The risk here is that success in selling at these prices may lead to increased orders, which may affect the company's earnings.

Spot price

The spot price is a price estimate for the quick settlement of a commodity. This settlement takes one to two days from the date of the trade. Spot pricing can forecast market expectations of future price schedules in many ways, depending on the traded item.

The spot price for a non-perishable product (such as gold) indicates market expectations of future price changes. The London Gold Fixing is a twice-daily telephone meeting between the representatives of five trading companies that determines the gold spot price benchmark.

In addition, active gold trading is backed by intraday gold spot prices derived from global gold markets. As with all other commodities, this price is determined by demand and supply. When considering selling your gold, the spot price is the very first thing you need to know.

Following the London Gold Fixing's decision and the demand and supply regulations, the rate is determined and converted to Euros, British Pounds and US Dollars.

Always, gold is measured in Troy Ounces. If the spot price of gold is £560, then one ounce of 24k gold is valued at £560 per ounce. You should not expect excessive profits if you decide to sell your gold.

The top gold dealers use a sliding scale for pricing. Some also pay 90% of the spot price. To anticipate a return, you must understand the game's rules.

When selling your gold scrap, there are many factors to consider and if you do not know what you are doing, it will be quite costly. Remember that the return rate should increase proportionately to the number of items sold.

Some people only sell a little amount of gold during their lifetime, while others pass it on to their heirs. If you enter a store with broken gold jewelry that you wish to sell, you must know the appropriate procedures and formulas; otherwise, you will lose everything without even realizing it.

Before selling your gold, you should always be well-informed on the subject. Before selling it, do a study or consult with an expert.

Many additional variables must also be considered when selecting and accepting the buyer's price. The price of gold is perplexing.

Always conduct research, even before selling scrap and attending a store. If you decide after entering the store and attempting to comprehend the pricing and everything else, you will take whatever the buyer provides.

Premiums

Making money is the ultimate goal but there are many routes to get there, so it is prudent to consider what else you wish to achieve.

Premium Pricing is often employed for products or services with a perceived high status; quality products with prestige have an assumed larger worth than their real monetary value and clients expect a high price as a result.

Using a premium pricing method signifies that the act of setting a high price can add value to the product or service, hence creating the desire to possess it.

If you want to increase your business's profits, one of the best things you can do is charge premium pricing. There are two significant causes for this. The first is that selling at a premium improves your profits immediately.

The second reason is that selling at premium rates makes it simpler to sell items because high price signals to the market that you have a high-quality product and most people choose quality over affordability.

Once, I had a client whose business struggled to generate a sufficient profit. After examining his goods and establishing that he was providing a substantial value, I advised him to raise his prices, not by a negligible amount, but to roughly double them.

He couldn't believe I was asking him to undertake something so extreme and it took me many weeks to convince him to give it a shot. After all, I said, you can always return the prices to their previous level if it fails.

So he attempted it. A few days following the price increase, someone visited his workplace for a product demonstration. Not only did the high price not affect sales but the prospect purchased the most expensive of the three versions available.

The prospect examined the three options, saw the most expensive one and desired only the best. In the years that followed, the customer was able to sell more things to a greater number of people than with any other strategy.

Rising prices augment demand.

This teaches us that high costs make consumers want your things more, not less, because most people want the best and want to believe they can afford it.

People who don't want the best and are unwilling to pay for it should be avoided at all costs, as they often moan about the price (even when it is low), pay late, make demands and overall make your life unpleasant. The greatest course of action is to send those individuals to your competitors.

Another advantage of premium pricing is that the additional money it generates is free and virtually directly turns into profits. Consider the matter carefully. If you increase your prices by 25 percent, that is money you did not have to work for. It truly is free money and the more you obtain, the better.

Lastly, you should remember that premium pricing is not limited to your standard offerings and items. It is also applicable to brand-new things.

If you have a large number of clients, it's almost certain that some of them will be willing to pay significantly more for the most expensive version of your product and the only way they can do this is if you manufacture and sell the goods.

In reality, every firm should have a deluxe edition to provide to its most valuable consumers and clients; failing to do so is a waste of money.

Greshams law

Gresham's law is the (previously widespread) observation that "bad money drives out good money." It occurred (and continues to occur in a sense) when governments compelled to overvalue one component of the money supply relative to the other (s). In the past, astute speculators who thoroughly understood this made a fortune; I believe it may do so again in the future.

During the peak of this law's popularity, most of the money supply consisted of gold and silver. Bimetallism policies often "decree" an exchange ratio between the two metals that overvalued and devalued the other.

Gresham's law predicts the inevitable consequence: the overpriced currency would rush into circulation, while the undervalued currency would be hoarded and traded overseas.

(Why? Suppose that you will soon be required to repay a debt and that the law permits you to do so with either gold or silver. In a climate where gold is overpriced and silver is undervalued, which would you choose?

Do you pay off the obligation with a greater quantity of silver or a lesser quantity of gold? You give away the least valuable item, a quantity of gold. Why spend more when it is possible to pay less?)

But why does this matter to investors/speculators/traders? I believe a modified version of Gresham's law is in effect today: "Bad money drives out good [so long as it is not extinguished]." Future postings will elaborate on what I mean by this statement.

Money is one side of every economic transaction. Like the ocean to fish, money is to things what money is to fish. A lack of money is related to an increase in the 'price' of money, whereas a surplus of money is associated with a decrease in that price.

In other words, when money is limited, prices decrease and when money is abundant, prices increase. Gresham's law can help us determine when significant changes in the money supply are likely.

If people have strong beliefs about the future that contradict monetary patterns (as outlined by Gresham's law), we can identify opportunities on the opposite side of their trades.

These transactions are likely to possess the coveted asymmetry: You won't lose anything if you're wrong (or if they're right) but you stand to gain greatly if you're right (or if they're wrong).

In the most fundamental sense, all businessmen participate in the exchange of money for goods and goods for money. They anticipate that their efforts will yield profits.

What if, in the meanwhile, the money supply is cut in half? Or suppose it doubles? Are individuals prepared for these opportunities?

72 rule

A straightforward method for determining how long an investment will require to double, given a set yearly interest rate. By dividing 72 by the yearly rate of return, investors can approximate the years required for the initial investment to double.

Typically, investments are evaluated based on a metric known as the "rate of return." Based on the rate of return, one can determine how much the investment earns per dollar after a specific period. For instance, an investor invests $100 in a savings account with a 3 percent yearly return.

After one year, the investor anticipates receiving $103. The investor might have chosen to exit from the investment much earlier, often resulting in a reduced return proportional to the investment's duration.

However, not all financial vehicles, such as CDs and savings accounts, carry interest. Government bonds and bank accounts are examples of those that do (and the CDs discussed above). The remainder of the financial instruments, including securities, stocks and high-yield mutual funds, lacks rates.

An investor who purchases a share of stock should anticipate a set return. Again, a hypothetical investor invests $100 to purchase firm shares. After a year, the value of these shares could be anywhere (within reason) and the investor could have lost money.

Mutual funds operate similarly to stocks because each fund comprises many types of stock. The fund's return will fluctuate in the same manner as it's component equities.

Given this information, some investors may now comprehend why financial institutions continue to advertise "fund rates." Some companies even advertise that they offer high yield mutual funds, yet the term high yield mutual fund is not well-defined.

The rates advertised by financial companies for their funds are historical rates of return. The "rates" of mutual funds with exceptional performance are typically touted.

The caveat is that the rate is entirely based on past data and the following year's rate may (or will likely) be substantially different. A historical rate indicates a fund's performance in the past but not necessarily its future performance.

Why do fund yields fluctuate in such a manner, sometimes declining in some years? One reason is that the value of the underlying securities (the stocks) constantly fluctuates as each company's fortunes change.

This is by far the greatest contributor to the volatility of the stock and mutual fund prices. Another factor is that firms often pay dividends.

Occasionally, a corporation with very large quarterly or annual profits will opt to reward its shareholders or those who hold stock. Profits provided as incentives are referred to as dividends, which typically raise the value of each fund share.

The most important thing to understand is that rates, such as those for stock, bond and GNMA mutual funds, are simply historical rates and are not comparable to rates for fixed income assets such as savings accounts, bonds and certificates of deposit. Funds with a high yield should likewise be regarded in this manner.

Relative value

This is a method for determining the value of an asset that considers the value of like assets. In contrast, absolute value solely considers an asset's inherent value and does not compare it to other assets.

Einstein's theory of relativity can also be applied to investment decisions in the stock market. In economic terms, this concept is referred to as "opportunity cost," as investing in one company costs you the return you might have earned by investing in another.

How can you maximize your decision and reduce its opportunity cost?

When picking between some market possibilities for investment, it is always essential to have a comparable ratio. When making informed investment decisions, using similar ratios becomes increasingly crucial as the stock markets expand and the fundamentals of all listed companies diverge greatly.

I have developed what I believe to be a solid comparable ratio (even across sectors). Let's call this ratio "Relative Value." The ratio attempts to identify the stock with the largest dividend yield and the highest undervalued growth rate.

Perform the following fundamental procedures for each firm:

Determine the share's Price Earnings (PE) ratio. The "Share Price" is divided by "Earnings per Share" in the table below.

Calculate the company's long-term growth rate (G). This single figure will be the most difficult to obtain and require extensive investigation and judgment.

If you lack the confidence to forecast your growth rate, you should contact your broker and get him or utilize the brokerage's census growth rate.

Price Earnings Growth (PEG) ratio calculation This represents "PE" divided by "G."
Calculate the share's Dividend Yield (DY). These are the dividends paid historically divided by the share price.

Finally, determine the share's Relative Value. This represents "Dividend Yield" divided by "PEG."

Can you see how the lower the PEG of stock, the less you pay per unit of the company's growth.?

In addition, the higher a stock's DY, the higher the dividend yield you will receive from your investment and the higher a stock's DY, the lower its PEG, the higher its Relative Value ratio.

If you wished to invest in Standard Bank (SBK) or ABSA (ASA) on the JSE Securities Exchange, for instance, you would use the symbol "SBK" or "ASA" (the South African stock exchange).

Standard Bank has a P/E of 8.38, a DY of 3.29 percent and a projected growth rate (average of brokers) of approximately 15%. Thus, the Relative Value ratio for Standard Bank is 6.98 (= (3.29 percent) / (8.38 / (15 percent x 100)).

ABSA has a PE of 6.81, a DY of 5.86% and a predicted growth rate of roughly 13% (according to the consensus of brokers). Thus, ABSA's Relative Value ratio is 11.19 (=(5.86 percent) / (6.81 / (13 percent x 100)) (=(5.86 percent) / (6.81 / (13 percent x 100)).

Therefore, ABSA appears to be the best alternative. It looks like you will receive a higher return on your investment due to a balance between dividends and capital appreciation.

Although the Relative Value ratio is useful for investors, it does not replace the necessity to investigate and comprehend each company's fundamentals before entering.

The Relative Value ratio requires many assumptions to achieve its objective of comparative investment analysis, with the utilization of historical data being the most significant. Remember that the past is not always indicative of the future and rely on your discretion when making decisions.

Intrinsic value

This is a technique for determining the worth of an investment based on its cash flows. In contrast to market value, which indicates the price others are prepared to pay for an asset, intrinsic value is derived from an analysis of the item's real financial performance.

A property's intrinsic value results from its predicted cash flows, growth and risk. Since gold is not a cash-flow generating asset, its intrinsic value cannot be estimated.

A corporation's intrinsic value reflects its assets' value and/or the cash flows generated by those assets.

In simpler terms, intrinsic value is the value of the business, as opposed to the present market price.

So why do we need to calculate the business's intrinsic value?

Here are four explanations:

1. To decide whether the stock price is affordable or costly

Suppose you wake up one morning to find that your favorite stock has gained 10% due to great earnings. The price has increased from $10 per share yesterday to $11 today.

You then assess the company's intrinsic value and determine that each share is worth $25. Then you examine the price and conclude that it is still inexpensive based on the business value. Thus, it is a purchase.

In contrast, if you calculated the stock's intrinsic value and determined it is worth $8 a share, you would sell it. At $11 per share, it is pricey. Therefore, it is not a buy; if you own shares, you should likely sell.

2. To understand anticipated returns

The objective of investing is to generate returns. In every investment decision, you must be aware of your expected returns. Once you have the stock's intrinsic value, it is simple to determine your return on investment.

Let's return to the preceding illustration.

If you determine that the stock's intrinsic value is at least $25 per share and the share price is $11, your return on investment is 127. The stock is an absolute steal!

3. To be aware of opportunity costs

We live in a world with many financial options. Should I invest in real estate, bonds or stocks? In stock market investing, there are many equities from various industries from which to choose.

How do we develop our portfolio?

We should invest in equities that provide greater returns for an appropriate degree of risk. If your desired yearly return is at least 15 percent, you should select investments that offer returns over that percentage.

If stock Alpha gives a 50 percent return based on the calculation of intrinsic value, whereas stock Beta only offers a 10 percent return, you should select Alpha.
Your investing decisions will after that be optimal and based on anticipated returns.

4. To establish your Safety Margin

The three most important terms in investing are "margin of safety." Ben Graham popularized the margin of safety as a technique for capital preservation. The concept behind this is that you should only purchase a stock if the price provides a substantial margin of safety relative to your calculated value.

Suppose the computed intrinsic value is $10 per share; if the stock trades at $9, you should not purchase it. You allow for an error margin in your calculations of value. Waiting until the share price falls to $5 before purchasing provides a 50% margin of safety in this situation.

Rate of return

The rate of Return is the "speed" at which you make money back annually, every year, forever, relative to the initial investment amount. So that it may be compared to the larger amount invested, it is expressed as a percentage (percent). For instance, if you invest $100 and receive $3 annually, the "rate of return" is 3%. Is it not so?

Now, let's alter the problem slightly. What if, on the same $100 investment described above, you gain money over some years but not the same amount each year?

And what if the cash flow could cease after a specific number of years? For instance, you will receive $5 for the first year, possibly $8 for the second year, $3 for the third year and $95 for the fourth year (which may also be the final year. so it is not forever). What is the current rate of return?

As you can see, calculating the percentage rate in this most recent instance is challenging. It is not as straightforward as in the first example since the annual cash flow is not a constant quantity (like $3 in the first case) and is not permanent.

This latest percentage is now known as the Internal Rate of Return. Since it is difficult to obtain the percentage, we can say that it is "hidden"; hence, the term "internal"; because "internal" is a formal way of stating "hidden."

How is this idea practical?
If the internal rate of return (IRR) of your project or business endeavor is lower than your cost of debt or the interest rate you would pay to a bank (if you borrowed money from the bank to finance the investment or project), then it is not a suitable investment.

Why? Of course! Because if you pay the bank 3 percent for a project or investment and it produces an IRR of just 2 percent, you lose 1 percent.

In contrast, if your IRR or Internal Rate of Return is more than the amount you would borrow from the bank to fund an investment or project, it is a smart investment due to the positive "spread" between your rate of return and cost of debt. Likewise, if your IRR equals the interest rate you would pay to the bank, you break even.

This is a condensed explanation of the internal rate of return. In more complicated situations, you can compare your internal rate of return to your cost of debt and your cost of equity or a weighted average cost of capital (WACC).

Velocity of money

Turbochargers have permanently changed aviation and auto racing by boosting engine performance and speed that earlier engine modification techniques did not permit.

In finance, improved dollar-for-dollar performance can be attained by utilizing the powerful concept of "Velocity of Money," in which each investment dollar is placed in many locations simultaneously to keep money circulating in a personal economy.

The "Velocity of Money" is a crucial aspect of the world of finance concerning the global economy. The Federal Reserve utilizes this model to assess the state of our economy. Every bank in the United States implements the "Velocity of Money" concept in their daily operations.

Local banks routinely utilize their strength. When banks get your funds, they do not simply let them sit idle. Instead, they invest it to generate further funds with the same initial sum; they never use the money for a single purpose.

"If an individual deposits $1 in a bank's savings account, the bank will invest that dollar in multiple areas to increase its wealth. Why wouldn't a person want to employ the same strategy?

Ultimately, the key to applying the velocity of money is to comprehend how an individual might invest his or her money "through" something, as opposed to "to" something "Lyons argues.

The "Velocity of Money" approach to accumulating money is a time-tested, multi-decade-old tactic. The phrase was coined in the 1930s by the mathematical economist Irving Fisher and referred to cash circulation in a given country.

Today, the finance and mortgage coaches at LEI apply this strategy to their clients' specific economies to establish a constant and reliable cash flow.
This worldview is founded on elementary mathematical equations. The theory is based on the exchange equation, which states:
$M \cdot V = P \cdot Q$.

To comprehend this equation in layman's words, one must first comprehend the phrases provided. M represents the amount of money in circulation within an economy.

V stands for the speed of money (how often each unit of money is spent). P is the economy's average price level for a given month and Q is the number of commodities purchased with the money represented by M during that month.

This equation demonstrates how "Velocity of Money" can be applied to your economy. The formula M and V in the equation represents the amount of money spent, while the sum represents the amount of money collected.

It boils down to adopting the straightforward procedure of putting your money to work by keeping your investment dollars in motion to generate additional financial benefits.

Zero sum game

HAVE YOU MET MONEY?

In game theory and economic theory, a mathematical description of a situation involving two sides in which the outcome is an advantage for one side and an equivalent loss for the other.

A zero-sum game is one in which the total amount earned by the winners matches the total amount lost by the losers. Gambling is an excellent example of a zero-sum game. In all games of chance, the pot of money at stake will be shared among the winners, losers and the house.

The house can theoretically be counted among the losers in any particular instance but gambling is often a profitable business since the house wins significantly more often than it loses. This implies that, as a group, gamblers often lose more than they win.

However, what is occurring is a redistribution of the wagering funds. The total amount gambled does not vary between the time the wagers are placed and the game's conclusion.

The ongoing debate has surrounded the question of whether investing in the stock market is a zero-sum game. Those who assert this point to the fact that every trade has a winner and a loser.

If an investor buys a stock and the price rises, he or she wins and the individual who sold the shares loses the same amount. (Transaction costs are omitted for the sake of simplicity.) The roles of winner and loser are flipped if the stock price falls.

Those who argue that investing in the market is not a zero-sum game point out that, as the market tends to gain in value over time, most investors are statistically destined to be winners if they maintain their positions for the long term.

According to our reasoning, both arguments are partially right but do not give the complete story. The second argument disregards the reality that when a seller cashes out a stock position and registers a large profit, the investor who buys the position theoretically incurs a loss because he or she might have purchased the stock at a lower price earlier.

The first argument ignores the reality that dividend payments increase the return on investment with a stream of income, raising the overall return for all investors beyond the simple capital gain of purchase and subsequent sale.

Investment time horizon

This is the length of time an investor plans to retain an investment before withdrawing funds. Investment objectives and techniques substantially determine time horizons.

People's "time horizons" mistake is most likely the greatest error they make in their financial planning. A financial time horizon is, by definition, the amount of time over which a sum of money is expected to be invested. If our time horizon is one year, we have fewer possibilities. However, if it is longer, we have more.

It is a part of human nature that as we age, our cognitive abilities diminish. If I were to suggest to a 75-year-old woman that she purchases a 15-year bond, she would not agree but based on life expectancy tables, my recommendation is reasonable.

To illustrate time horizons, I will use the example of U.S. Treasuries. I inform the prospect that they have additional possibilities if they look longer.

"Mrs. Jones, US Treasuries are the safest location to keep your money. However, if you do not search for longer, you will not obtain the increased rates.

A one-year Treasury may only yield 1-2 percent, whereas a ten-year Treasury may yield 4-5 percent. We have so many more alternatives due to our extended search."

The example I presented previously is clearly understood. Once a prospect comprehends their option in connection to their objectives, it makes perfect sense to sell them the appropriate product.

We offer longer-term goods and describe the safety of our products in the same manner as we would for U.S. Treasuries. Putting our items in the same category as other safe and secure products instills confidence in our customers.

Diversification

Diversification is the process of diversifying your investments such that your exposure to any one sort of asset is limited. This strategy is intended to lower the portfolio's volatility over time.

Diversification is a way of mitigating risk by distributing a portfolio's funds among many investment categories. These classifications are known as "asset classes," and selecting how much to invest in each asset class is known as "asset allocation." Diversification is based on the premise that a portfolio including different investments will yield greater returns with less risk than one containing only a few items.

Why You Need Diversification

Suppose you have only one investment in a huge insurance firm. Years later, tornadoes in the Midwest destroyed tens of thousands of homes.

Later, two major hurricanes struck Florida and the Gulf region. The potential claims are so large that the insurance firm may go bankrupt and its stock price plummets. Your portfolio is in tatters.

Suppose, however, you had invested half of your money in an insurance company and the other half in a home improvement and building supplies company, rather than investing all of your money in a single insurance company. In this case, the storm damages would decrease the value of your insurance stock.

Still, residences would need to be rebuilt or repaired, driving up demand for construction materials and the value of your investment in the building materials company.

Because these two stocks appear to counteract each other, a statistician would say they do not have a significant "correlation" or similar behavior.

When constructing a diverse portfolio, we want asset classes that not only behave differently but also have a certain degree of "inverse correlation," meaning that if some investments decline, others will rise to balance losses (stocks and bonds often move in opposite directions).

This is why diversification mitigates your chance of loss. The more you diversify your portfolio with asset classes that are inversely correlated, the more likely you are to reduce risk.

Asset management

Many of you have likely heard the word "asset management" before but you may not fully understand its meaning. Management of assets is a broad concept.

It can be characterized as a process that directs the acquisition of assets and their use and disposal so that the assets and their potential are maximized throughout their useful lives.

In addition, it manages and maintains any associated costs and risks with the assets. It is not something that can be purchased but rather a discipline that must be adhered to preserve your assets.

Asset Management can be utilized for many purposes. Most employ asset management to track their cash or "liquid assets." In addition to investments, banking institutions are considered a form of asset management (savings accounts, certificates of deposit, mutual funds, money market accounts, etc.).

Another example of an asset is the product that firms offer. These items are considered to be assets. Using the proper asset management system, the product can be made more accessible, simpler to produce, less expensive to distribute to clients, etc.

Asset Management Resource:

Asset management also entails monitoring and insuring the product. The product is an asset to the company and vital to its continued existence and financial health. Therefore, the maintenance and management of this product are of the utmost importance.

Many individuals do not consider another form of an asset when they hear the phrase "asset management." This asset relates to public and shared assets, including the construction and maintenance of streets, highways, water treatment facilities, sewage, electricity, natural gas and clean air. All these are necessities for everyone on the planet. Typically, your city or local government employs asset management to keep track of the cost of these assets.

Also, they use it to create some of these assets more effectively and economically. Managing natural resources such as water, electricity and natural gas ensures that they are regularly renewed and hence inexpensively accessible.

Asset Management Resource:

There are many methods for managing assets. Often, it depends on the sort of asset involved. Companies and software packages support asset management. Regardless of the technique you select, your asset management system should include the following elements:

1. Maximize the accuracy, dependability and efficacy of the assets to optimize their use and manage their maintenance activities;

2. Utilizing demand management approaches and sustaining current assets to reduce the demand for new assets and save money.

3. Utilizes a sort of asset tracking: knowing at all times where the asset is, how much it is worth and how much it originally cost. This should also be incorporated for the duration of the asset's life.

4. Seeks to maximize the return on investment by examining the asset's maintenance, production and utilization costs, etc.

Always give a report detailing the value of the assets and any costs associated with their maintenance.

Hopefully, you can better grasp the various asset management methods. So many items might be considered assets; thus, there are so many distinct asset management strategies.

Now that you have a better understanding, you can determine your assets and how you may better preserve them so that they are more advantageous to you!

Compound Annual growth Rate

This is the annualized average revenue growth rate between two specified years, assuming growth occurs at an exponentially compounding pace.

HAVE YOU MET MONEY?

Compounding is one of the most effective strategies to improve your wealth. Using the power of compounding requires only fundamental knowledge and discipline; the rest is taken care of automatically.

This sectiiion is useful for individuals who have a basic understanding of investments, a steady income and, most importantly, financial aspirations of financial independence and immense wealth!!! We will cover passive saver/investor statistics and the need for discipline.

Einstein stated accurately that compounding is one of the most potent forces of the twenty-first century. I believe that his comment applies to this century as well. Add discipline and money management to your financial independence plan and you are well.

As always, discipline is essential for whatever success we hope to accomplish. As we know from the pay-yourself-first strategy, the foundation of any financial independence is removing some money off the top.

The portion of one's salary that he or she attempts to save for financial independence can range from 1% to 50% of one's income, at the discretion of the individual. Let's crunch some numbers for fun and the beauty of compounding will become clear.

How can one increase their net worth by savings and investments to at least one million? A few highly pertinent points that can be observed and deduced are:

Increasing CAGR (compound annual growth rate) increases returns. Why is this statement so obvious? This is the essence of financial independence.
More money saved or invested yields greater returns. This is another fundamental concept of financial freedom that we often overlook.

Long-term thinking rather than short-term gratification is the only way to reach one's financial objectives. The significance of starting early or as quickly as feasible.

With the same 15 percent CAGR, the total amount invested over 30 years is only 3.6 lakhs and the return is 56.32 lakhs, which is approximately double the return on a monthly investment of 10,000/- over 10 years!!!

As the CAGR rises, the danger steadily grows as well.

An annual inflation rate of 6% wipes up a portion of your earnings. Thus, the return is drastically reduced and is rather low; therefore, instrument 1 of the chart is ruled out.

For passive investors, there should be a balance between higher growth returns and safety. I've chosen the term passive investor because once he receives the requisite fundamental information and advice, he leaves his savings/investments to his bank or fund manager and adheres to his financial plan.

This passive investor/saver is a cut above the usual individual who doesn't have time for his financial goals and leads a directionless existence while hoping to become wealthy by coincidence or luck. Utilize the immense power of compounding to create mega-wealthy and permanent financial independence.

Compound Interest

It would appear that compound interest is the most perplexing of all the financial words in the world. Maybe the word or the method used to calculate it causes many to misinterpret how compound interest works.

Compound interest does not have to be confusing, though; the information below should answer most, if not all, of your questions regarding compound interest and how it can influence you.

What Is It?

The term "compound interest" refers to the practice of earning interest on both the initial principal and the interest that has previously been applied to it.

This means that the amount of interest compounded each time is added to the principal for the next time interest is applied on the amount (also known as compounding).

Simply put, compound interest means that each time interest is charged, it is based on the whole amount rather than just the principal.

What Is Its Purpose?

Since compound interest is applied to all the funds stored within the compounded account, this means that, as time passes, more funds will accrue within the account as each rise increases the amount being paid. This is frequently the case with savings accounts and interest-bearing checking accounts and with interest due on many loans.

How Is It Determined?

$A = P(1 + r) n$ is the formula for calculating compound interest, where A is the amount of money amassed after the interest has been compounded, P is the principal deposit amount, r is the annual interest and n indicates the number of years during which interest is collected.

If the interest is compounded more frequently than once a year, r is divided by the frequency at which the interest is compounded (for monthly interest, this would be 12 times and for the daily interest it would be 365 times.)

Imagine that P is 100 based on a monthly compounding rate of 5 percent interest for 5 years. This expression would appear as A = 100(1 + 5/12) 5 or 100 x (1 + 5/12) with the section in brackets multiplied by itself five times.

How Do You Benefit From It?

Since compound interest pays extra interest depending on the interest that has already been paid, over time you will make a substantial amount of money simply by keeping your principal in a savings account or other bank account.

Many banks and other lenders employ compound interest on their loans, so the longer it takes to repay the loan, the more you will have to pay back. This can motivate to repay debts during a grace period or at least to pay off the debt as quickly as feasible to save as much money as possible.

Locating the Best Prices

To obtain the greatest loan rates, it's essential to compare shop and examine your many alternatives regarding the type of account or loan you're seeking. Request rate quotations and compare them to guarantee that you receive a satisfactory rate and the lowest possible rate.

Due diligence

This is an investigation of a potential investment (such as stock) or goods to confirm all facts. These facts include evaluating all financial records, prior company/asset performance, and anything else deemed material.

If you intend on purchasing or selling a business, you need to consider due diligence as part of your plan and there are many components you must examine.

Why Is Due Diligence Significant?

Due diligence is vital as it allows one to develop a subjective judgment and analyze the facts. This is sometimes a lot easier said than done and the grade of work utilized in due diligence needs to relate to the reasons you are buying a business and what you may consider the primary risks.

Being a purchaser or entrepreneur intending to buy a small business, you are entitled to access any financial documents and research related to the company's transaction.

There are various procedures one can follow to ensure the proper information is accumulated and that it can conform to a minimum average so that you can make the final selection.

By completing the due diligence process, you need to grasp the general financial health of the company you seek to purchase, its leads, levels of competition and the present market.

Here Are Some Due Diligence Recommendations To Follow

The following list of points to address is not in any particular order. These are merely ideas and you may request additional information regarding the type of company.

1. An Action Plan for Due Diligence - all parties must agree on what issues and significant information must be supplied to conduct due diligence.

This includes but is not limited to the company's organizational structures, shareholdings, yearly legal reporting, personnel, legal and related groups and financial records.

2. Examine the financial statements - It is essential to examine the profit-and-loss accounts, balance sheets, annual reports and any cashflow statements. Validate all files with an accountant and the IRS to ensure they are complete and accurate.

3. Examine tax records - For Australian firms, it is crucial to obtain the income tax returns for the past three years and to assess each company activity statement (BAS).

In addition, ensure that their tax records correspond with their profit-and-loss statements and that all applicable taxes, including payroll tax, stamp duties and GST, have been paid.

4. Assess the assets - if there are any, examine the machinery and equipment to ensure they are in excellent working order. Perform a stock valuation before the day of settlement.

It is also advisable to study insurance information and facts to determine whether they have it covered till the agreement is finalized.

5. Analyze the scale of the prospects and suppliers; request a review of the list of major clients and ascertain whether or not they are active purchasers. Determine whether there are existing contracts and whether they will generate future recurring business.

Check their vendors to discover if there are any outstanding payments or invoices awaiting settlement. Check to discover if any unanticipated expenses may arise after you purchase the firm.

6. Determine why the owner is selling - find out why the business is being offered for sale and how long the owner has been in business.

Ask the buyers and suppliers, as they might also divulge additional information on the company.

7. Evaluate the amount of competition - Evaluate the level of competition to see if they will affect your business if you decide to take them on. Investigate any prospective dangers and industry developments.

8. Verify legal rights and investigate any government restrictions that may affect the business. Consult with an experienced attorney who can provide additional information on the legal factors that will affect the business.

9. Agree on a timeline for the due diligence - to limit the expenses and impact on the business, there must be a timetable for the due diligence to be completed. Typically, it should take no longer than twenty days.

Sign a Non-disclosure Agreement (NDA) between both parties; it is also advisable to have any necessary parties, such as an accountant, lawyer or consultant, sign an NDA. This will protect you and the company's assets during the due diligence.

Consider getting the files mentioned above and data from an online storage facility to ensure the system's consistency and success. This will make it easy to locate and access in future years. Consider saving this on Dropbox or Google Drive.

Then, you may provide specific individuals access to some or all the data and monitor their activity. Ensure that each document is systematically numbered and labeled so you can easily locate and refer to it.

It is incredibly advantageous to maintain due diligence data because it can be utilized in the future. Consider reading our website's due diligence guide if you're looking for further information that will assist you in deciding to purchase a small business.

Return on Investment

Return on investment or ROI, also known as return of capital or ROC, is the payments paid to the owners of the capital. These payments have outpaced the business's expansion. In this context, expansion refers to the entire enterprise's net income or taxable income.

Technically, this can be calculated by subtracting the investment's cost from its total return. The difference is multiplied by 100 and divided by the investment's cost.

This result is expressed as a percentage. To increase the reliability of the results in light of the fluctuating value of money over time, one can reduce a certain percentage of the overall cash flow.

The fundamental value of a return on investment (ROI) ratio is in its capacity to help measure the overall profitability of a firm. It demonstrates how efficiently a company spends its capital to maximize revenues. This is often favored due to the simplicity of computation and result interpretation.

When evaluating investments, those having a higher rate of return on investment are seen as more successful. As a result, they are preferred above alternative options for continuous operation. All other investments with a negative or null return on investment are a waste of time and resources.

Most individuals avoid or disregard the requirement for ROI computation and analysis. They have no idea what a grave error this is.

When evaluating multiple company options, it is essential to calculate the ROI. It assists the investor in determining which investment will be more profitable and, thus, more desirable.

In the case of larger organizations, a return on investment can help a shareholder evaluate the management's ability to utilize money and produce profitable results.

It is all about the management's ability to divide the money, allocate it to the many demands of the organization and generate profits.

Versatility is one of the characteristics of the formula for computing ROI. It is easily adaptable to the specific requirements of the individual investors concerned.

However, the substance of an ROI calculation is never lost during the calculating process. It is a metric used to evaluate the total operational capacity of investment.

Preparing for investment requires a thorough evaluation and study of the return on investment. In addition, it is a useful instrument for assessing which investments perform better than the rest of the crowd.

Opportunity Cost

This is the worth of what is forfeited when choosing between two or more alternatives. It is a fundamental principle of investing and of life in general. Opportunity cost is the amount of money you may not gain by acquiring one asset instead of another when investing.

When a business owner examines a Profit & Loss Statement, the items that affect the cost of running a business are evident: salary, rent, utilities, inventory purchase price, etc.

What is more challenging to perceive are what accountants and business consultants refer to as "Opportunity Costs."

Opportunity cost is the money or other rewards lost while pursuing a certain course of action rather than a mutually incompatible alternative." In other words, if you choose Option B, you forfeit any benefits that would have resulted from pursuing Options A or C.
As a manager or business owner, you desire to reduce Opportunity Costs. You accomplish this by evaluating the advantages and disadvantages of EACH of the available options.

This enables you to understand each alternative thoroughly and choose the one that best meets your immediate (and maybe intermediate) demands. Once the decision has been made, proceed.

When it comes to business funding, most business owners and top executives fail to consider Opportunity Costs. Why? I believe this is because they tend to emphasize the quantifiable cost of money more than the various costs connected with business finance.

Let me clarify. Opportunity Costs are not limited to monetary or monetary expenditures. They also properly include:

Sales not pursued

Vendor discounts not taken

Lost time (time spent chasing one funding opportunity while another alternative might have been concluded more quickly - this results in the executive's time being wasted, which can lead to lost profits)

Emotional influence on the proprietor(s), the proprietors' families, employees and their families (stress associated with business finance issues has implications on many levels)

HAVE YOU MET MONEY?

These are extremely real but intangible factors; since they are intangible, the temptation is to disregard or minimize their impact on the organization's financial health. This is an enormous, albeit understandable, error.

When underwriting a deal, practically all financial institutions (both traditional and non-traditional) will concentrate on the numbers.

They are required to do so because they are evaluating risk. Therefore, it is logical that the borrower would focus on "the numbers." That is the measurable expense of money.

Unfortunately, relying solely on figures nearly always causes one to overlook Opportunity Costs, which can be enormous. I've witnessed far too many owners postpone action for weeks to save a quarter of a percent on expenses.

Often, the delay caused revenue and profit losses that were orders of magnitude more than the cost of money. They were penny clever and pound foolish, to paraphrase an old proverb.

Opportunity Cost is not always simple to calculate in financial situations. This is because most banks and financial institutions refuse to participate in the analysis.

After all, they are attempting to seal the transaction, so they will emphasize the benefits of their specific course of action, regardless of whether it is the optimal answer for you at the moment.

The owner/executive is responsible for evaluating his/her Opportunity Costs. Paying a slightly higher money price to obtain funds quickly enough to seize an opportunity may be the optimal choice. What good is it to save $1,000 on the cost of money if you lose $10,000 in additional profit?

Tax loss harvesting

Selling stocks at a loss might reduce your tax liability on capital gains. Your capital gains and losses are netted against one another at the end of the year.

Your short-term gains are taxed at the same rate as your ordinary income. Long-term gains are typically taxed at 15%. There is no annual limitation on the number of losses used to offset realized gains.

Also, you can deduct $3,000 in realized losses from your ordinary income. Any residual losses can be carried forward indefinitely to subsequent tax years. These tax losses carryforwards may be utilized to lower future capital gains or to offset $3,000 of your annual ordinary income.

This process need not be completed at the end of the year. This can be done at any time during the year. You can be able to incur losses at the beginning of the year that is unavailable at the end of the year.

Many factors to consider: heed the IRS Wash Sale Rule with caution. This rule stipulates that security cannot be sold and repurchased within 30 days. If you do so, you will cannot deduct the loss from your taxes. In addition, losses made in retirement plans or IRAs cannot be used to offset gains in taxable accounts.

Mutual funds and ETFs (Exchanged-Traded Funds) are typically more convenient than individual stocks for tax loss harvesting.

Here are a few instances:

You can sell Fidelity Select Health Care (FSPHX) and purchase the Vanguard Health Care Fund (VGHCX) to retain a similar level of exposure without having to wait 30 days or accept a loss. You can sell SPY (S&P 500) and purchase IYY (Dow Jones U.S. Index Fund).

Tax professionals advise against selling one index fund and purchasing the same index fund from a different fund company. It is preferable to purchase a different index using the proceeds.

If done correctly, tax loss harvesting can decrease your tax liability and come close to preserving the original structure of your portfolio. This post is intended solely for educational purposes and should not be considered personalized investment advice.

Risk management in finance

Financial risk is a circumstance in which the return on a specific investment decision is very low. It is possible to lose the entire or a portion of the financial gain of an investment. Some risks are manageable and can be avoided, while others are completely unavoidable and lead to a certain loss.

Financial managers use financial risk management to improve a firm's economic value and collateral management by decreasing its exposure to external risks, such as credit and market hazards. This strategy employs various financial choices.

The term "risk" refers to the probability that an undesirable outcome will occur due to a present decision or a few future occurrences. In life, we face a vast number of these dangers.

Sometimes there are risks that we are willing to take, while there are others that we try to avoid and sometimes there are risks that we believe are worth taking and others that we do not want to consider since they are certain to result in a loss.

In terms of risk-taking, the world of finance and business is not significantly more sophisticated than our everyday lives. During a company endeavor, managers or investors must confront obstacles.

As in ordinary life, some of these risks are easily manageable while others are not and the method of determining financial solutions is part of the risk management process.

Risk management describes identifying, examining, analyzing and treating company risks. However, as businesses encounter different hazards, many risk management specializations have been developed to address them.
Enterprise risk management is a subfield of risk management that educates about non-financial issues.

Then there is financial risk management, essentially similar to general risk administration with a financial focus. Similar to fundamental risk management, this topic emphasizes risk recognition, analysis, evaluation and follow-up. It focuses more intently on finances and banking solutions and utilizes financial instruments to mitigate the enterprise's risk.

Instead of providing entrepreneurs with different options, financial risk marketing focuses mostly on hedging, adopting two counterbalancing investment strategies that mitigate the effects of price volatility. Aside from these differences, the remainder is nearly identical.

Risks are inherent to any company endeavor; thus, when it comes to financial risks, businesspeople have no choice but to manage them.

For this reason, understanding financial risk and its management are crucial in the corporate sector. The technique will not aid businesspeople in avoiding risk but will allow them to evaluate the impacts of risk whenever they need to make a decision.

Therefore, it helps you to comprehend the industry better. It teaches you about collateral management, how to invest in a field and how much may be lost if the investment fails. Nevertheless, the market dangers are avoidable.

Ratio of total debts to total assets

When an entity, whether a corporation or a person, wants to know where it is financially, one of the best ways to do so is to create financial statements.

A crucial component of a financial statement is a comprehensive and detailed accounting of a person's or company's assets and obligations to determine their liabilities-to-assets ratio, which can shed light on whether their financial path is heading to riches or debt.

In addition to financial statements, a balance sheet is a valuable financial report that can provide a fast snapshot of the financial health of a business, individual or family.

Typically, a balance sheet will include all the property or present assets that contribute to wealth accumulation. These total assets include equities and bonds, real estate equity, cash on hand and other liquid assets, dependable cash flows, tools and equipment and intellectual property.

The liabilities column of a balance sheet indicates the current debts and financial commitments owed to third parties.

In addition, when calculating the liabilities-to-assets ratio, some accountants include items that are often overlooked, such as pending taxes, professional licensing and required fees to remain in business, obligations entered into via contracts and other types of arrangements that require an eventual transfer of current assets to a third party.
A basic illustration of calculating the ratio between liabilities and assets can be shown by examining an individual's position.

The current assets of a homeowner would include the home's fair market value, deposits in all checking and savings accounts, the portfolio of all shares, stocks and bonds and investments in gold, silver, other coins, stamps, artwork, fine jewelry and similar items of value that typically increase in value over time.

In addition, total assets may also comprise retirement money, projected pension rights, and any recurring payment promissory note.

For individuals, the listing of total assets may also include various sorts of personal property. These other assets may include automobiles, boats, leisure vehicles, tools and implements, household furnishings and even apparel.

However, these are the types of commodities that degrade in value over time. Thus, some accountants eliminate them from a balance sheet to accurately depict true household wealth.

The liabilities column of a balance sheet indicates the current debts and financial commitments owed to third parties.

In addition, when calculating the liabilities-to-assets ratio, some accountants include items that are often overlooked, such as pending taxes, professional licensing and required fees to remain in business, obligations entered into via contracts and other types of arrangements that require an eventual transfer of current assets to a third party.

Personal Financial plan

A personal financial plan consists of six fundamental steps:

1. Assess your present financial status

2. Establish your financial objectives

3. Determine different routes of action

4. Evaluate alternatives

5. Develop and implement your financial strategy

6. Examine and amend the financial plan. There is never a bad time to begin planning.

Personal financial planning is essential and one of the most essential things you can do is to create a solid budget. Every aspect of your financial life should be considered. If you do not plan your spending carefully, your financial planning may end in tragedy.

Finding a quality budget spreadsheet or computer application is an excellent starting point. Many free websites provide these tools for personal financial planning, but not every program is suitable for every individual.

You require a worksheet or program that considers all areas of your spending. There are many small items that you might not consider including. A quality application will organize these for you.

Set aside a certain amount for savings and retirement when preparing your budget. Even if you can only afford to save $5 or $10 every month, it will be beneficial to do so.

You will enjoy the satisfaction and security of watching your savings account increase as you save small sums. Many banks even offer to set up a monthly automated transfer from your checking account to your savings account. This is an excellent tool for personal financial planning.

Before you can construct a budget, you must complete some tasks. You will need to collect your bills, bank statements and pay stubs.

This will ensure that your financial planning is efficient and that you do not have to search for bills and bank statements continually. You will also have a clearer understanding of your financial situation.

Ensure that your budget includes all of your income streams. Even if you earn money through investments or side employment, you must include this income on your tax return. Personal financial planning is only effective when attention is paid to the particulars.

After listing your revenue, you should subsequently list all your costs. This is the most difficult aspect of personal financial planning for most people. Consider all of your expenditures, not just the major ones. The cost of regular lattes may quickly build up and derail even the best-laid plans. However, if you are honest with your budget, you can prepare for these minor luxuries and remain financially on track.

A budget should be a dynamic instrument for personal financial planning. Your lifestyle will alter, as will your expenditures. A monthly budget review can help you stay on target and make any required adjustments. This will give you peace of mind and allow you to live within your means.

A budget is the most significant personal financial planning tool accessible. While some may view it as restricting, it might provide you with the financial independence you require.

You will be aware of how much money you possess and how much you can spend. As you can see, it is simpler than you may believe to begin personal financial planning.

REFERENCES

Boyes, William J., and Michael Melvin. Economics. 7th ed. Boston: Houghton Mifflin, 2008.
Becker, Gary, Human Capital: A Theoretical and Empirical Analysis. Chicago: University of Chicago Press, 1993
Cecchetti, S.G. (2008). Money, Banking and Financial Markets (2nd edition). New York: McGraw-Hill Irwin.

Currie, L. (1934). "The supply and control of money in the United States," Chapter XV. Harvard University Press

Case, Karl E., Ray C. Fair, and Sharon M. Oster. Principles of Economics. 9th ed. Upper Saddle River, NJ: Prentice Hall, 2009.

Colander, David. "The Art of Teaching Economics." Middlebury College.

Colander, David. "What Economists Teach and What Economists Do." Middlebury College.

Colander, David. "What We Taught and What We Did: The Evolution of the US Economic Textbook (1830-1930)." Middlebury College. Web.

Chen, M.-H. (2010). Understanding world metals prices-Returns, volatility and diversification. Resources Policy, 35(3):127–140

Eddie McLaney: Business Finance: Theory and Practice. 8th Edition, Pearson Education

Frank, Robert H., and Ben Bernanke. Principles of Economics. 4th ed. Boston: McGraw- Hill/Irwin, 2009.

Friedman, Milton and Rose D. Friedman, Capitalism and Freedom. Chicago: University of Chicago Press, 1972

Hall, Robert Ernest, and Marc Lieberman. Macroeconomics: Principles & Applications. 5th ed. Australia: South-Western Cengage Learning, 2010.

Krugman, Paul, and Robin Wells. Microeconomics. 2nd ed. New York, NY: Worth, 2009.

Mankiw, N.G. (2010). Macroeconomics, seventh edition. New York: Worth Publishers.

Marshall, A. (1890). Principles of Economics. London: Macmillan and Co

McLeay, M., Radia, A., and Thomas, R. (2014a). "Money creation in the modern economy." Bank of England Quarterly Bulletin, 54(1):14-27

McConnell, Campbell R., Stanley L. Brue, and Sean Masaki. Flynn. Economics: Principles, Problems, and Policies. 18th ed. Boston: McGraw-Hill Irwin, 2009. Print.

Miller, Roger LeRoy. Economics Today. 15th ed. Boston: Addison-Wesley, 2011. Print.

Nowman, K. B. and Wang, H. (2001). Modelling commodity prices using continuous time models. Applied Economics Letters, 8(5):341–345.

North, Douglas C. Economic Growth in the United States: 1790-1860. Seattle: DIANE Publishing Co., 2003

Radetzki, M. (1989). Precious metals - The fundamental determinants of their price behaviour. Resources Policy, 15(3):194–208

Saunders, Phillip, and William B. Walstad. The Principles of Economics Course: a Handbook for Instructors. New York: McGraw-Hill, 1990.

Schiller, Bradley R. Essentials of Economics. 7th ed. Boston: McGraw-Hill/Irwin, 2009.

Skousen, Mark. "The Perseverance of Paul Samuelson's Economics." Journal of Economic Perspectives—Volume 11, Number 2—Spring 1997—Pages 137–152.

Stiglitz, Joseph E., and Carl E. Walsh. Economics. 4th ed. New York, NY [u.a.: Norton, 2006

Taylor, N. J. (1998). Precious metals and inflation. Applied Financial Economics, 8(2):201–210

Thurow, Lester, The Future of Capitalism. New York: Penguin Books, Inc., 1997.*

Urquhart, A. (2016). How predictable are precious metal returns ? European Journal of Finance, To Appear(0):1–24.

Vivian, A. and Wohar, M. E. (2012). Commodity volatility breaks. Journal of International Financial Markets, Institutions and Money, 22(2):395–422

Varela, O. (1999). Futures and realized cash or settle prices for gold, silverm and copper. Review of Financial Economics, 8:121–138.

Withers, H. (1909). The meaning of money. London: Smith, Elder & Co

www.ingramcontent.com/pod-product-compliance
Lightning Source LLC
Chambersburg PA
CBHW031616210526
45464CB00004B/1605